Whispers of Warriors

Whispers of Warriors

Essays on the New Joint Era

by Ike Skelton

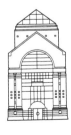

NATIONAL DEFENSE UNIVERSITY PRESS
WASHINGTON, D.C.
2004

Library of Congress Cataloging-in-Publication Data

Skelton, Isaac Newton.
    Whispers of warriors : essays on the new joint era / by Ike Skelton
        p. cm.
    Includes bibliographical references.
    ISBN 1–57906–071–4
    1. United States—Military Policy. 2. United States—Armed Forces. 3. Military art and science. 4. World politics—1995–2005. I. Title.
    UA23 .N5428 2004
    355.4′6′0973—dc22

                                                 2004061085

First Printing, December 2004

NDU Press publications are sold by the U.S. Government Printing Office. For ordering information, call (202) 512–1800 or write to the Superintendent of Documents, U.S. Government Printing Office, Washington, D.C. 20402. For GPO publications on-line access their Web site at: http://www.access.gpo.gov/su_docs/sale.html.

For current publications of the Institute for National Strategic Studies, consult the National Defense University Web site at: http://www.ndu.edu.

Contents

Foreword

This collection of articles by the Honorable Ike Skelton represents the author's deep and abiding commitment to the Armed Forces of the United States. As the ranking Democrat on the House Armed Services Committee, he has been an acknowledged leader in defense affairs in a lifetime of public service. As chairman of the panel on professional military education, Mr. Skelton helped implement the provisions of the Goldwater-Nichols Act of 1986, which had a profound impact on staff and war colleges. As the National Defense University has grown into a center of excellence in joint education, Congressman Skelton has been an active supporter of our programs. In recognition of his efforts, the university awarded him its first honorary degree, a doctorate in national security affairs, in 2001.

In his contributions to military journals, Mr. Skelton has demonstrated an understanding of military history, leadership, and education. Many of those articles are gathered herein. They offer still-pertinent ideas for meeting the challenges of the war on terrorism, enhancing jointness, and transforming the military. The 12 articles, which appeared in the pages of *Aerospace Power Journal, Joint Force Quarterly, Military Review, Naval War College Review, Parameters*, and *Strategic Forum*, are published by the National Defense University both as a service to the military community and as a tribute to their author.

Michael M. Dunn
Lieutenant General, U.S. Air Force
President

Preface

In an essay I wrote a few years ago (chapter 8 of the current volume), I reminisced about my childhood fascination with the hat that my father wore as a sailor during World War I and how it connected me to his military past, of which I am still so proud. Throughout my career as a Congressman and as a proponent of joint professional military education, I have come to view that hat as much more than a childhood curiosity: that hat represents all of our pasts as Americans; it speaks of the countless told and untold stories of warriors who have given so much to ensure our freedom today and tomorrow.

Only by studying and reflecting on these stories of warriors can we move securely into the future. This is why I have written a number of essays in support of educating the joint warfighter strategically, operationally, and historically. At the international level, the United States must remain engaged with allies and coalition partners in pursuing its strategic goals; at the operational level, U.S. forces need to be trained in and aware of the cultures of allies and enemies alike. A thorough mastery of military history, furthermore, is essential for any military professional because the past has important lessons to teach about warfighting skills, tactics, leadership, innovation, and strategy. Effective commanders, I believe, are ones who can capitalize on those skills in extreme and stressful situations to ensure the well-being of their soldiers and successful accomplishment of their mission.

I have always been a strong advocate of teamwork, which is especially important for the Armed Forces today as they train and fight to win the war on terrorism. Because warfare changed so drastically after the end of the Cold War, the needed emphasis on joint professional military education, especially at the mid- to senior-level military colleges, has never been greater. The challenge continues to be how to maintain one's warfighting proficiency in the fast-paced, technologically advanced, multidimensional battlefield on which we find ourselves. Indeed, future leaders must continue learning from the past to build an even more effective force that can deal with challenges such as urban warfare, weapons of mass destruction, and ongoing operations.

This book is a compilation of articles written since the early 1990s, most of which have been published in various professional military journals to include *Military Review* and *Joint Force Quarterly*. In addition, I have included as an appendix a recommended list of readings to enhance the joint warfighter's continuing professional military education. This volume was made possible by the Institute for National Strategic Studies at the National Defense University (NDU), which expressed interest in publishing, under one cover, this series of articles. NDU Press—George Maerz, Lisa Yambrick, and Dr. Jeffrey Smotherman—brought it to completion under the supervision of Colonel Debra Taylor, USA, Managing Editor, and Robert A. Silano, Director of Publications. I want to thank them all for their long hours and hard work. Finally, thanks go to my colleague in the House of Representatives, Jim Cooper, who co-authored chapter 12.

Whispers of Warriors

Chapter 1

Joint Professional Military Education: Are We There Yet?

In late 1987, the Panel on Military Education of the House Armed Services Committee began its review of joint education at the command and general staff colleges of the four services. We issued our preliminary recommendations in November 1988 and our final 206-page report in April 1989.[1]

The panel recommended the establishment of a two-phase joint specialty officer (JSO) education process as part of a wide-ranging series of recommendations concerning intermediate and advanced professional military education.

The panel recommended that phase one be provided to *all* students attending a service intermediate college. We made this recommendation because we strongly believed that officers of all four services at the major/lieutenant commander and lieutenant colonel/commander ranks should have an understanding of, if not expertise in, multiservice matters—*jointness*. Familiarity with doctrine, organizational concepts, and command and control of the forces of each of the services was to be included in the curriculum of all four service intermediate schools. In addition, the students would be introduced to the joint world—the joint planning processes, joint systems, and the role played by service commands in the unified command structure.

We recommended that phase two, the detailed, in-depth course of study in the integrated deployment and employment of multiservice forces, be accomplished at the Armed Forces Staff College (AFSC), Norfolk, Virginia. The idea was that only the small percentage of intermediate

---

This chapter originally appeared as the lead article in *Military Review* (May 1992).

school graduates en route to assignments as joint specialists would attend the AFSC. They would build on the knowledge they had gained during the phase one course of study.

I am pleased to report that this key recommendation of our panel, the establishment of a two-phase JSO education process, was enacted by the Department of Defense. As proof, some of those now attending the course of study at the U.S. Army Command and General Staff College (USACGSC), Fort Leavenworth, Kansas, or at another service's staff college will, upon graduation, proceed to Norfolk to attend the AFSC.

Service Expertise First

The Goldwater-Nichols Department of Defense Reorganization Act of 1986 did much to promote the concept of jointness among the four services. Likewise, our panel's efforts have gone far in promoting jointness in the area of professional military education. We realized that one of the ways to promote better joint planning and joint operations was through professional military education and the development of the JSO. (The other important tool for improving joint operations is for the services to sponsor more joint training exercises.)

However, we also recognized that the successful JSO first had to be an expert concerning his or her respective service. While each of the four intermediate service schools now has a role in promoting joint education, each one still has the primary function of educating officers to become competent in their respective warfare specialties. The USACGSC, for example, must provide Army officers a firm foundation on the merging of separate Army branch elements into integrated Army combined arms forces that can conduct land warfare with the support of air and naval forces. This is to be done at the operational level.

An Army officer must thoroughly understand the capabilities, characteristics, strengths, and weaknesses of Army forces. He or she must have a very good understanding of the integration of combat, combat support, and combat service support elements employed in the conduct of successful Army operations.

The opening shots of the air campaign during Operation *Desert Storm* were fired by Army Apache attack helicopters. Their mission succeeded in destroying a number of Iraqi early warning radar sites. The success of the mission allowed coalition aircraft to surprise the Iraqi air defense forces on the first night of the war. This was crucial in allowing the coalition air forces to gain air supremacy. Their losses that first night over Iraq were zero.

The story behind the story was one of interservice cooperation. While the Army possessed the attack helicopters that took out the radar sites with laser-guided Hellfire missiles, it was U.S. Air Force special operations aircraft, MH–53J Pave Low enhanced configuration helicopters, that acted as pathfinders for the Army choppers. As General H. Norman Schwarzkopf sought recommendations from his staff, Army officers needed to understand the navigational limitations of the AH–64 Apache. On the other hand, Air Force officers on the commander in chief's (CINC's [combatant commander's]) staff needed to know that Air Force special operations Pave Low helicopters could provide the navigational guidance lacking in the Army attack helicopters.

This example illustrates the requirement for JSOs on joint staffs to be experts on their respective services. An Army infantry JSO would have needed to understand the capabilities and, more specifically, the navigational limitations of Army AH–64s. Similarly, an Air Force fighter pilot JSO would have needed to know that the Air Force had in its inventory not only fixed-wing aircraft but also Pave Low special operations helicopters able to help the Army AH–64s overcome their navigational limitations for the crucial mission against the Iraqi early warning radars.

Jointness and Joint Education at the Command and Staff Colleges

Our panel report listed the attributes of the JSO—a thorough knowledge of his or her own service, some knowledge of the other services, experience operating with other services, trust and confidence in other services, and the perspective to see the "joint" picture. Ultimately, a JSO must "understand the capabilities and limitations, doctrine and culture of the other services."[2]

Joint education at the command and staff colleges of the four services has come a long way since our panel began its work. Last year, we held hearings to assess the progress made by the various intermediate- and senior-level schools to implement the recommendations we had made. Prior to the hearings, we asked the General Accounting Office (GAO) to assess the implementation of these various recommendations. The GAO report on the two Army schools (USACGSC and the U.S. Army War College) came out in March 1991. It noted that the USACGSC had implemented or partially implemented 29 of 31 recommendations.[3] The next month, the panel had the opportunity to hear Major General John E. Miller, USACGSC deputy commandant, discuss the progress made on implementing our panel's recommendations 2 years earlier.

CGSC Situation Report

The story on joint education at intermediate-level military educational institutions is a positive one, not simply for the Army but for all the services. Each has in place a phase one course. At Fort Leavenworth, the effort has been one to include the phase one material throughout the six blocks of instruction. I have had the opportunity to examine the curriculum from the previous academic year and can see the amount of time devoted to joint matters. My instincts tell me that the balance of instruction between land-force capabilities and joint capabilities is about right. And I believe that it is done in the proper fashion—more Army-specific courses in the early part of the curriculum, with greater attention to joint issues toward the end of the course.

It would be interesting to hear from both faculty and students whether they also believe the balance between Army and joint matters is just about right. I am sure that if there are concerns about this issue, letters touching on the subject will appear in future issues of *Military Review*. Those who would want to write me directly are encouraged to do so.

Another positive development at Fort Leavenworth concerns the increased number of sister service students attending USACGSC. Both the Air Force and the Navy have increased the number of students at the school. This academic year, the Air Force total was scheduled to reach the 80-student mark. This coming fall, the naval services will also reach the 80-student mark (60 Navy and 20 Marine).

The Navy has been able to improve both the number and quality of students at Fort Leavenworth because of our panel's efforts to have the Navy provide more line officers to other service intermediate and senior schools. This was a cooperative endeavor on the part of both our panel and the Navy. I believe that we have been successful. This means that there should be a greater number of Navy officers in the seminar groups that meet throughout the year at USACGSC.

Four years ago, not every seminar had a naval officer. Others that did had officers who were either lawyers, supply officers, or others who would never command a ship, a submarine, an aviation squadron, or some larger combat formation.

Student/Faculty Mix

Yet our panel was somewhat disappointed that its recommendations for student and faculty mix of officers from the three military departments were not followed. The first recommendation called for intermediate service schools to have student body mixes of two officers from each of the two nonhost military departments in every student seminar. This was to be achieved by academic year 1995–1996. So, at Fort Leavenworth, that would mean that in each seminar there would be two Air Force officers and two Navy officers (or one Navy officer and one Marine officer).[4]

Our faculty mix recommendation at the intermediate level called for 80 percent from the host school and 10 percent from each nonhost school military department. We called for its implementation by academic year 1990–1991. By academic year 1995–1996, the comparable figures were to have been 70 percent and 15 percent from the other two military departments.[5] In both the student and faculty mixes, the recommendations of our panel were relaxed by the Military Education Policy Document (MEPD) issued under the guidance of the Chairman of the Joint Chiefs of Staff in May 1990. The MEPD sets guidance in the area of joint education. While its recommendations set the minimum levels in the matter of both student and faculty mixes, the USACGSC viewed those minimum levels not as floors but as ceilings. While the situation of student and faculty mixes is better today than it was 4 years ago, it is not as good as our panel believes it could be.

Study of Military History

Another area that our panel report stressed was the study of military history, especially in helping to develop strategists. In our visit to Fort Leavenworth in 1988, the study of military history was confined to 51 hours and limited to the American experience of war in the 20th century. Army officers, especially those who will rise to command at the corps or theater level, need a thorough understanding of military history that reaches back over the ages.

The recent war in the Persian Gulf exhibited elements of campaigns fought in previous wars. I am confident that Schwarzkopf's familiarity with those campaigns, through his study of military history, helped him design the strategy that resulted in the overwhelming victory of the allied coalition over Iraq. The lessons for him to draw upon could be found in military actions spanning more than a century.

The 6-week air campaign allowed American and coalition aircraft to pound away at Iraqi installations and forces so that when the ground campaign finally went forward, resistance was comparatively light. Maybe the World War II battle of Tarawa acted as a cautionary tale about halting a bombing campaign too early. During that amphibious landing, Marine forces suffered heavy casualties because the island had not been hit hard enough with air and naval gunfire.[6]

The placement of Army and Marine forces along the border between Saudi Arabia and Kuwait was reminiscent of Sir Bernard L. Montgomery's North African Campaign, which used deception to defeat the German Afrika Korps at El Alamein.[7] And, finally, the famous "left hook" that struck with such force and surprise against the right flank of the Iraqi ground forces may have derived its inspiration from our own Civil War. At the Battle of Chancellorsville, General Robert E. Lee, too, dispatched forces under General Thomas "Stonewall" Jackson around the right flank of General Joseph Hooker's Union troops and routed them in a manner that was daring and aggressive.[8]

These examples of how history may have been used in *Desert Storm* simply underscore the point that a profound understanding of military history is crucial for any officer attending the U.S. Army Command and General Staff Officer Course at Fort Leavenworth. Since our panel visit in early 1988, the course has broadened its study of military history to include 18th-century warfare. The seeds of future American military victories can be found by plowing deeply the fertile soil of military history.

Military Education in the 1930s

During the Great Depression of the 1930s, in a far harsher budgetary climate than that of today, all of the services found themselves reduced to "pauperdom." The sizes of the forces were drastically cut, and modernization programs were, at first, postponed and then canceled. The Army, which during the Great War had numbered more than 2.3 million, was reduced to less than 138,000 by 1934. In a crisis, the Army could have fielded 1,000 tanks, all obsolete; 1,509 aircraft, the fastest of which could fly 234 miles per hour; and a single mechanized regiment, organized at Fort Knox, Kentucky, led by horse-mounted cavalrymen who wore mustard gas–proof boots. The United States had the 16th largest army in the world, with Czechoslovakia, Turkey, Spain, Romania, and Poland possessing larger armies.[9]

Too poor to train and equip their forces, the Army, Navy, and Marine Corps took advantage of a difficult situation by sending their best officers to various schools to study, teach, and prepare for the future. The Infantry

School at Fort Benning, Georgia; the Command and General Staff School at Fort Leavenworth, Kansas; the Naval War College at Newport, Rhode Island; the Army War College in Washington, DC; and the Marine Corps schools at Quantico, Virginia, experienced a renaissance.

It was during the interwar years, the "golden age" of American military education, that such renowned World War II military leaders as George C. Marshall, Dwight D. Eisenhower, Joseph Stilwell, Omar N. Bradley, Chester W. Nimitz, Raymond Spruance, and Henry "Hap" Arnold benefited from study at intermediate- or senior-level war colleges. William F. "Bull" Halsey, Jr., who commanded the Central Pacific amphibious campaign against the Japanese during World War II, attended *both* the Army and Naval War Colleges. Marshall taught at the Army War College and was the assistant commandant of the Army Infantry School.

During this same period, the Marine Corps devoted considerable effort at Quantico, its seat of learning, putting together the doctrine of amphibious warfare used to such telling effect, from Guadalcanal to Okinawa, in the Pacific campaigns of World War II. The naval-oriented Fleet Marine Forces became the spearhead of the Navy's Orange Plan, the basic outline for executing a war against Japan, which was adopted in 1926. The best summation for the period was made by Nimitz, who noted that the entire Pacific campaign had been thought out and fought in the classrooms of the Naval War College during the 1930s. The only unforeseen event was the use of kamikaze suicide aircraft attacks on U.S. Navy warships during the latter stages of the Pacific war. In short, we won the victories of the 1940s in the command and staff and war college classrooms of the 1920s and 1930s.

Military Education in the 1990s

Shifting from the recent past to the more uncertain future, I want to touch on the important task of educating our country's military leaders, present and future. A first-rate officer education program—from lieutenant to general—will prepare today's military officers for tomorrow's challenges by providing them the most important foundation for any leader—a genuine appreciation of history. I cannot stress this enough because a solid foundation in history gives perspective to the problems of the present. And a solid appreciation of history provided by such a program will prepare today's military officers for the future, especially those who decide to spend 30 years in one of the services. They will become this country's future strategists.

In the March 1989 issue of *Parameters*, the U.S. Army War College quarterly, General John R. Galvin, supreme allied commander, Europe, describes why our country needs strategists in each of the services and at all levels. "We need senior generals and admirals who can provide solid military advice to our political leadership," he writes, "and we need young officers who can provide solid military advice, options, details, the results of analysis to the generals and admirals." He lists three elements in an agenda for action:

- formal schooling
- in-unit education and experience
- self-development.[10]

In brief, the military student should learn the historical links of leadership and be well versed in history's pivotal battles and how the great captains won those battles. Successful military leaders of yesteryear were indebted to their military predecessors. Jackson's successful Shenandoah Valley campaign resulted from his study of Napoleon's tactics, and Napoleon, who studied Frederick the Great, once remarked that he thought like Frederick. Alexander the Great's army provided lessons for Frederick, 2,000 years before Frederick's time. The Athenian general, Miltiades the Younger, who won the Battle of Marathon in 490 BC, provided the inspiration that also won the Battle of El Alamein in 1942; the Macedonian, Alexander the Great, who defeated the Persians at the Battle of Arbela in 331 BC, set the example for the Roman victory at Pydna 155 years later. The English bowmen who won Crecy in 1346 also won Waterloo in 1815; Alexander A. Vandegrift, Bradley, Montgomery, or Douglas MacArthur, who won battles in the 1940s, might well win battles a century or so hence. Thus, I believe that every truly great commander has linked himself to the collective experience of earlier generals by reading, studying, and having an appreciation of history.

A military career includes a lifelong commitment to self-development. It is a process of education, study, reading, and thinking that should continue throughout an entire military career. Yes, tactical proficiency is very important, but so too is strategic vision. That can only come after years of careful reading, study, reflection, and experience. Those at the USACGSC who finish their course of study should be aware of the natural yardstick of 4,000 years of recorded history. Thucydides, Plutarch, Sun Tzu, Carl von Clausewitz, Napoleon, Alfred T. Mahan, and Sir Halford John Mackinder have much to offer those who will become tomorrow's future generals and admirals. Today's officer corps must be made aware of this inheritance.

Winston Churchill put this idea in these words: "Professional attainment, based upon prolonged study, and collective study at colleges, rank by rank, and age by age ... those are the title reeds of the commanders of the future armies, and the secret of future victories."[11]

A Joint School of Advanced Military Studies

As I survey the past 4 years, I see much progress that has been made in fostering joint education at the four intermediate service schools and at the AFSC. The recent publication of Joint Publication 1, *Joint Warfare of the U.S. Armed Forces*, underscores the efforts of the services to promote jointness.[12] In many ways, our panel's work simply reinforced and accelerated trends that had already been under way in the services.

Professional military education is an important element in the development of tomorrow's senior military leadership. The Army established its School of Advanced Military Studies (SAMS) in 1983 to provide the Army with officers specially educated for military operations. It is expected that the graduates of this 1-year follow-on course of the intermediate command and general staff course will become the commanders and general staff officers of the Army. Cross-pollination has worked to the extent that both the Marine Corps and Air Force have established equivalent courses (the School of Advanced Warfighting for the Marine Corps and the School of Advanced Airpower Studies for the Air Force).

One idea that merits serious study is the establishment of a Joint SAMS course under the auspices of the AFSC. It would be similar to the follow-on schools at Fort Leavenworth, Quantico, and Maxwell Air Force Base, Alabama, but would have a joint focus. Such a school would seek applicants from graduates of the four command and staff colleges.

The details of such a course need to be worked out. Here are some suggestions. The student body should initially be composed of 60 officers, 20 from each military department. They may even be AFSC graduates who stay on for further study. Such a school would allow the Chairman of the Joint Chiefs of Staff and the unified commanders to have a pool of officers well grounded in the planning and conduct of joint operations. It would be a course of study that would be added to rather than supplant the current second-year courses found at Fort Leavenworth, Quantico, and Maxwell. One advantage of such a course would be to have Navy participation.

In 1923, Major George C. Marshall, the future World War II Army chief of staff, described the regular cycle in the doing and undoing of measures for the national defense. He observed that "we start in the making of adequate provisions and then turn abruptly in the opposite direction and abolish what has just been done."[13] Today, we are in the midst of making one of those changes in direction.

World conditions have changed, the Cold War is over. The challenge now is to reduce the size of our military effort without putting at risk our national security. There are still threats to American interests in the world that cannot be ignored.

While Americans want a reduction in military spending, they do not want to reduce spending in such drastic fashion that we risk undoing all the hard work and money spent since 1980 in restoring the military. Americans also understand George Washington's wise counsel, "To be prepared for war is one of the most effectual means of preserving peace."[14] I am convinced that they will support measures needed to maintain an adequate and credible national defense in order to preserve the peace that we enjoy today.

But these next few years for those in the military will be difficult ones nonetheless. As we reduce the size of the services, professional military education should not be forced to take its "fair share" of the cuts. The fact is that smaller forces will have to be more capable forces. That means continued high levels of training and efforts to improve professional military education. Doing business in a joint fashion will become even more necessary.

Eisenhower got it right more than 30 years ago when, in a message to Congress, he noted, "Separate ground, sea, and air warfare is gone forever. If ever again we should be involved in war, we will fight it in all elements, with all Services, as one single concentrated effort. Peacetime preparation and organizational activity must conform to this fact."[15] Building on the accomplishments of the past few years, the enactment of the Goldwater-Nichols Act in 1986 and the greater effort in both service and joint professional military education will allow us to have a greater chance for securing a lasting peace.

Notes

[1] U.S. Congress, House Armed Services Committee Panel on Military Education, "Report of the Panel on Military Education," 101st Congress, April 21, 1989.

[2] Ibid., 55.

[3] "Army: Status of Recommendations on Officers' Professional Training," briefing report to the Chairman, Panel on Military Education, House Armed Services Committee (Washington, DC: U.S. General Accounting Office, March 1991), 2.

[4] "Report of the Panel on Military Education," 128.

[5] Ibid., 127.

[6] Robert Leckie, "Strong Men Armed: The United States Marines Against Japan," in *Illustrated History of World War II* (Pleasantville, NY: Reader's Digest, 1984), 236.

[7] Bernard L. Montgomery, "The Memoirs of Field Marshal Montgomery," in *Illustrated History of World War II* (Pleasantville, NY: Reader's Digest, 1984), 292.

[8] Peter Batty and Peter Parish, *The Divided Union: The Story of the Great American War, 1861–1865* (New York: HarperCollins, 1997).

[9] William R. Manchester, *The Glory and the Dream: A Narrative History of America, 1932–1972* (Boston: Little, Brown and Company, 1974), 6.

[10] John R. Galvin, "What's the Matter with Being a Strategist?" *Parameters* 19 (March 1989), 2.

[11] "Report of the Panel on Military Education," 12.

[12] Joint Publication 1, *Joint Warfare of the United States Armed Forces* (Washington, DC: National Defense University Press, 1991).

[13] George C. Marshall, "The Effect of School Histories on National Defense," in *Report of the Tenth Annual Conference of the Association of Military Colleges and Schools of the United States*, Washington, DC, 1923.

[14] John Bartlett, *Familiar Quotations* (Boston: Brown, Little and Company, 1968), 461.

[15] Edward C. Meyer, "The JCS—How Much Reform is Needed?" *Armed Forces Journal International* (April 1982), 84.

Chapter 2

Joint and Combined Operations in the Post–Cold War Era

Three years ago, prior to the disintegration of the Soviet Union, former Secretary of Defense Richard B. Cheney, General Colin L. Powell, Chairman of the Joint Chiefs of Staff (JCS), and their respective staffs crafted a new National Military Strategy.[1] The new strategy envisioned the end of the Cold War. It differed from the earlier Cold War strategy in many ways. First, it saw the primary threat as regional rather than global. Possible confrontations with Iraq, Iran, and North Korea occupied the attention of planners rather than a possible world war with the Soviet Union. Second, the new strategy also emphasized conventional forces rather than nuclear weapons. For example, the Air Force reconfigured much of its bomber force for conventional use in regional crises. Third, forward presence replaced forward deployment as one of the key policies by which to secure American interests around the globe. Overseas basing would be significantly reduced, and intermittent presence would be increased. The American military would become a primarily continental United States (CONUS)-based force, especially the Army and Air Force.

The base force, as articulated by Department of Defense (DOD) officials, accompanied the new military strategy and called for reducing the size of all four military services.[2] It envisioned roughly a 25-percent reduction in the size of American military forces and the size of the defense budget by the middle of this decade.

Author's Note: I wish to express my gratitude to Major Mary F. O'Brien, USAF, for her insight and research contributions in the preparation of this article, which was originally published in *Military Review* (September 1993).

The New World Disorder

In the midst of these plans—in fact, on the same day that former President George Bush was giving a major speech on the new National Military Strategy in Aspen, Colorado—Iraqi armed forces invaded and occupied Kuwait on August 2, 1990.

The ensuing Persian Gulf War was a stunning victory. Sailors in the gulf, soldiers and marines ashore, and airmen in the skies defeated a brutal foe. All of the world witnessed the great skill, determination, and professionalism of the American military. Among other things, the war showed that our investment in quality people, tough training, and first-rate weapon systems, both combat and support systems, in the 1980s was money well spent. Those who fought in the gulf helped write another magnificent chapter in American military history.

Despite the end of the Cold War, the Kuwait invasion and the subsequent war revealed that the world was still a dangerous and uncertain place. The kaleidoscope of the future is still unpredictable.

The end of the Cold War has been accompanied by a resurgence of nationalism—in some places, militant nationalism. This resurgence poses a major challenge to the established political and economic order. The disintegration of states—Yugoslavia, the Soviet Union, and Ethiopia—will generate conflict about the distribution of assets.

This is the fourth great wave of state creation since the end of the Napoleonic Wars in 1815. The first was in Latin America after the withdrawal of Spanish power; the second occurred in Europe and the Middle East after the collapse of the Austro-Hungarian, Turkish, and Russian empires. The third took place after World War II, when Britain, France, and the Netherlands relinquished control of their respective empires, some more willingly than others. The end of communist rule in what was the Soviet Union marks the fourth great period of state creation. In short, the world will not be a particularly stable place.

The fault lines of international security are shifting in many directions: Eastern Europe has now become Central Europe; Southwest Asia has given way to Central Asia. The continued utility of military force for good or evil has not been eliminated, nor have the principles of deterrence (conventional, as well as nuclear) lost strategic relevance. But the nonmilitary aspects of security—social, economic, and political—will now assume greater importance in the strategist's appreciation of the forces at play.

The Services Reorganize

In the midst of these momentous political developments, the service departments began their respective efforts to reorganize for the future.

Air Force

The Air Force issued its white paper, "Global Reach—Global Power," in June 1990.[3] This visionary document outlined a strategic planning framework for the Air Force in the post–Cold War era. Such venerable institutions as the Strategic Air Command, the Tactical Air Command, and the Military Airlift Command passed into history. The Air Combat Command incorporated all the winged firepower of the service—fighter, bomber, reconnaissance, command and control (C^2), tactical airlift, and rescue aircraft. Air mobility command acquired most of the mobility and refueling assets—strategic transport aircraft, tankers, and medical evacuation aircraft. Other changes included the streamlining and elimination of organizations. The Air Force will reduce the number of major commands from 13 in June 1991 to 8 by October 1993.

More than a fundamental management reorganization of the Air Force, "Global Reach—Global Power" symbolized a new way of thinking for airmen. Artificial distinctions between tactical and strategic were done away with, and airpower is now considered as a unified whole. At the same time, the Air Force discovered some old truths that have been important to the Army as an institution for many years—the importance of professional military education (PME) and, closely tied in with education, the importance of doctrine.

Navy

The Navy, the service that traditionally has been most resistant to change, has also responded to the end of the Cold War and its experience in the Persian Gulf War with its own white paper, ". . . From the Sea."[4] Issued in September 1992, after about a year's study, the new strategy incorporated two assumptions. First, the authors of the new strategy believed that the United States and its allies would have uncontested control of the seas. Second, they thought that most future military operations would be "joint," involving more than one service.

The document symbolized a new way of thinking for the Navy in a number of respects. The focus for future operations has shifted from the open sea to the coastlines of the world. In close cooperation with the Marine Corps, the emphasis on littoral warfare "is a new doctrine that marries Navy and Marine forces and priorities. . . . The Navy and Marine

Corps will now respond to crises and can provide the initial, 'enabling' capability for joint operations."[5]

Similar to the Air Force approach, the Navy also accompanied its change in strategy with a change in structure. The staff of the Chief of Naval Operations (CNO) was rearranged on a functional basis to mirror the organization of the JCS. The new CNO organizations conform to the JCS' J–1 through J–8. Power has shifted from the three separate baronies—air, surface, and submarine warfare—to the new N–8, the deputy CNO for resources, warfare requirements, and assessments. Rather than dividing budgetary resources into roughly equal shares as in the past, the new arrangement allows one individual to control the money flow. As a result, the Navy has already made plans to try to protect amphibious and carrier assets by reducing the attack submarine fleet by half and retiring all 35 *Oliver Hazard Perry*–class frigates. Similar to the Army and Air Force, the Navy has finally come to understand the importance of doctrine. It will establish a naval doctrine command to help smooth the integration of Navy and Marine Corps forces in a joint power-projection role, building doctrine for expeditionary warfare.

Army

In many ways, the Army instituted a number of far-reaching changes 20 years ago, in the waning years of the Vietnam War. The outcome of that bitter conflict was reflected in three crucial decisions that affected the Army more than any other service—the end of the draft and beginning of the All-Volunteer Force (AVF), the creation of the Total Force concept, and the establishment of the U.S. Army Training and Doctrine Command (TRADOC), Fort Monroe, Virginia.

Although many military leaders expressed great misgivings about the AVF, by the early 1980s the services had finally learned how to make it work. Recruiting high school graduates and paying them well helped create the Army of Excellence that proved itself in Panama and Iraq. The importance of the Total Force concept was also vindicated in the Persian Gulf War. Since much of the Active Army combat support and combat service support was found in the Reserve components (RCs), the requirement to activate those forces helped bring along the support of the American public. It worked just as Army Chief of Staff Creighton Abrams had designed it back in the early 1970s. And the third decision, the creation of TRADOC, revealed the U.S. Army in the deserts of the Middle East fighting with the synthesis of excellent people, first-rate equipment, and top-notch military thinking for the employment of forces.

While less prone to issuing white papers showing the great changes it is undertaking, the Army is indeed undergoing fundamental changes as it shapes itself as a strategic force for the 21st century. The Army is coming home. It will be primarily a CONUS-based force rather than the forward-deployed force it was during the Cold War. In addition to substantial force reductions that have produced the inactivation of four divisions and one corps along with the consolidation of 51 war reserve stocks to 5, the Army has recently issued the latest version of U.S. Army Field Manual (FM) 100–5, *Operations*, its bible. Understanding the new world in which it finds itself, the Army has seen fit to include a chapter on "Operations Other Than War." One need only read today's newspapers to see Army forces involved in such operations in Zagreb, Macedonia, Somalia, northern Iraq, and Latin America to see the need to address such contingencies.

Although there is no Army version of "Global Reach, Global Power" or ". . . From the Sea" that the service can point to as a blueprint for the future, FM 100–5 is a major step in the right direction. However, more needs to be done to explain the Army's future.

While each of the services is reorganizing for the post–Cold War era, each understands that most military operations in the future will be joint, multiservice efforts. This viewpoint has been underscored by the November 1991 release of Joint Publication 1, *Joint Warfare of the U.S. Armed Forces*. This publication and the related effort to develop joint doctrine will help the services to work more closely together in a period of declining budgets and force structure. There will be room for leading thinkers from each of the four services to offer their creative talents for melding the disparate ways the services think about the employment of their respective forces. The recent publication of *Joint Force Quarterly*, under the auspices of the Institute for National Strategic Studies at the National Defense University, is still another indication that jointness has finally come of age.

While the services have been busy adjusting to the changing political circumstances of the world since the fall of the Berlin Wall in 1989, the Chairman of the Joint Chiefs of Staff has also been busy reviewing defense policies. Earlier this year, as a result of the Goldwater-Nichols Department of Defense Reorganization Act of 1986, the chairman issued the latest report on "Roles, Functions, and Missions of the Armed Forces of the United States." Two considerations predominated in the effort to put together the report: improving the way the Armed Forces fight, and saving money in the process.[6] The report noted the dramatic changes that have taken place already: the creation of the U.S. Strategic Command; the elimination of nuclear weapons in the Army and Marine Corps; and the end of the requirement to maintain chemical weapons because of the signing by the United States of the Chemical Weapons Convention in Paris in January 1993. The report also highlighted the savings that can take place by further consolidation among the four services in the matter of depot maintenance and flight training.

Other changes on the horizon include the creation of a unified command for all units of the four armed services based in the United States, and the possible consolidation of space and strategic commands. Yet two of the key issues that were raised by the chairman of the Senate Armed Services Committee, Sam Nunn, in a significant speech July 2, 1992, were not addressed in the report of the chairman: the trade-offs between land-based versus sea-based power projection (Air Force bombers versus Navy carriers) and the ambitious tactical aviation modernization programs of the Air Force and Navy (four separate aircraft when there may be funds for only two at most).[7]

Testifying before the House Armed Services Committee in March 1993, Powell described the roles and missions report as "simply a snapshot of a continuous process of self-evaluation that occurs every day. The Joint Staff will continue to examine other areas for possible consolidation or elimination."[8] The Joint Staff will not be the only group involved in this effort. The Congress, think tanks, and other defense specialists will also be studying the matter of roles and missions. The end of the Cold War and the dramatic reduction in the size of U.S. military forces have ensured that this issue will be around for the next few years. In much the same way that the issue of defense reorganization took time to gather steam in the 1980s—from 1982, when former Chairman of the Joint Chiefs of Staff David Jones called for dramatic change, until late 1986, when the Goldwater-Nichols Act became law—it will take a few years to deal with the issue of roles and missions.

Arrival of a New Administration

The arrival of any new administration in Washington signals change. This is especially so with the election of President Bill Clinton, who promised change during the campaign. He is the first individual elected to the presidency born after World War II and the first President to begin his term of office after the end of the Cold War. His choice of Les Aspin, the former chairman of the House Armed Services Committee, as secretary of defense meant that one of Washington's leading defense thinkers would now be in the position to institute many of the changes he had promoted in his former position in Congress.

The new secretary signaled his effort to institute change almost immediately upon assuming office. He did so by redesigning the Office of the Secretary of Defense (OSD) and choosing a high-powered team of seasoned defense intellectuals to assist him. OSD has always been considered the weakest of the bureaucratic players at DOD, taking third place to the uniformed service staffs and the newly strengthened joint staff. A second and maybe more important effort was the "bottom up review" to chart the course for national defense for the future. The secretary has given a series of speeches explaining the overall effort of reducing defense spending and force structure, yet maintaining an adequate defense capability to secure American global interests.

One of the early trial balloons that got shot down quickly was the proposed strategy to fight two regional wars on a sequential basis. Known as "Win-Hold-Win," the strategy called for fighting a first regional conflict while essentially using air power to hold off a second adversary. Once the first regional conflict was won, those forces would then be redeployed to help win the second regional conflict.

Criticized, justly in my opinion, by some as "Win-Hope-Win" or "Win-Hold-Lose," the strategy seemed reminiscent of the mistake made by President Harry S. Truman's administration. In a major policy statement at the National Press Club in early 1950, Secretary of State Dean Acheson left South Korea outside the American defense perimeter in the Pacific.[9] The House of Representatives compounded the mistake by rejecting (193 to 192) a defense assistance program that would have provided 500 Army officers to supervise the equipping of South Korean troops.[10]

Joseph Stalin, dictating North Korean war plans, interpreted the American statement as a green light to begin preparations to invade South Korea. Obviously, the Truman administration had not intended, by way of Acheson's speech, to encourage North Korea to attack the south in its effort to reunify the peninsula. Yet that was the unintended consequence of the speech.

Similarly, Aspin would not want to encourage a second regional adversary to attempt to take advantage of a situation in which American forces were engaged in a regional conflict elsewhere. Why telegraph one's weaknesses?

Upon reflection, the secretary came to the same conclusion:

> After much discussion and analysis, we've come to the conclusion that our forces must be able to fight and win two major regional conflicts. . . . First . . . we don't want a potential aggressor in a second region to believe that we're vulnerable. Second, we want to be prepared in case an adversary emerges with larger or more capable forces than today's regional powers.[11]

Equally important, the secretary has talked about the importance of maintaining a strong peacetime presence of U.S. military forces around the world. He recognizes the fact that such presence contributes to regional stability, sending the signal that the United States is committed to protecting American and allied interests. And yet the dilemma we face is doing all this with a military force structure that is shrinking. The secretary admits that "creative thinking" will be needed. Some of the ideas being considered are rotating Air Force squadrons to forward bases for limited periods; having Navy ships, Air Force long-range bombers, and Airborne Warning and Control System aircraft operate together as part of the same joint task force; and conducting more but smaller military exercises with allies.

If nothing else, the new Aspin defense team is wrestling with some very tough issues. The new DOD leadership realizes that as the American military reduces in size it must maintain its readiness and remain a quality force, ready to fight. It has identified the three major challenges to readiness:

- maintaining good people in the military
- keeping up training and maintenance
- ensuring the proper esprit de corps.

Truth be told, the American military establishment is under great stress. The reductions experienced by each of the services caused turbulence and uncertainty. In addition, the debate over removing the ban on homosexuals serving in the Armed Forces has caused great anxiety among those in uniform. And the recommendation in the proposed fiscal year (FY) 1994 defense budget not to include a cost-of-living allowance increase is penny wise and pound foolish and sends the wrong signal to those in uniform. At the end of the day, I believe that the Congress will take action on homosexuals and pay, which will find favor among the vast majority of servicemembers.

The new secretary made evident his commitment to readiness by the appointment in May of a high-level readiness task force of eight retired flag officers. Headed by former Army Chief of Staff General Edward "Shy" Meyer and including former Army Vice Chief of Staff General Maxwell Thurman, the group will help the secretary make sure that we do not return to the "hollow force" of the late 1970s. It is a move that I strongly support.

The two most successful secretaries of defense since World War II have been two former members of Congress—Melvin Laird and Cheney. The former helped maintain military strength at a time of reduction during a most difficult period, our extended withdrawal from Vietnam. The second managed the difficult task of cutting forces while fighting a major war in the Middle East.

They possessed a broad understanding of security issues along with an intimate understanding of Congress. The current secretary has all the makings of being able to follow in their footsteps and maybe even surpass them. He, too, understands Congress every bit as well as his distinguished predecessors. But his knowledge and understanding of security issues at the outset of his appointment as secretary of defense far surpasses those of Laird and Cheney when they assumed office. Aspin has spent more than 25 years preparing for this opportunity, with service as a DOD analyst and later in Congress. With the support of both the President and the Congress, both of which I am confident he will get, he can help this country move toward a substantially smaller military in reasonably good shape. It will be a very difficult task to accomplish, but if anyone can do it, Aspin can.

Proposals to Maintain and Strengthen the Military

Peering into the future is not easy, but some outlines on the horizon are visible. First, we know that defense spending will continue to decline over the next few years. Second, the world remains a dangerous place despite the disappearance of the Soviet Union, so the need for capable American military forces remains. Third, joint operations among the services and combined operations with friends and allies will more and more characterize future American military efforts as we seek to maintain American military power despite force reductions.

Among the various proposals to maintain military capability, I would include the following. First, the Army needs to continue improving the relationship between its Active and Reserve components. Much that is positive has happened, including the Army's *Bold Shift* initiative and the Title XI Army National Guard Combat Reform Initiative in the FY 1993 Defense Authorization Act. More needs to be done, especially in the area of reserve PME. If more responsibilities are to be placed upon RC forces, they must be provided greater opportunities to become more proficient through PME.

An even greater opportunity awaits the Army if it views the RC combat units as a genuine asset to be developed rather than as simply another requirement it must address. Such units could be fashioned as building blocks to allow the Army to expand the number of divisions in case a hostile world-class military power arises over the next generation—a fascist Russia or an expansionist China. Many Army personnel who are leaving the service may be just the kind of people that the Army could place in such RC units in order to have an officer and noncommissioned officer corps made up of experienced personnel. The Army would do itself a great service to look at another ground-oriented fighting force, the Marine Corps, to copy some of the elements that have made the Active-Reserve relationship among marines a very healthy and effective one.

These are very difficult problems to address because of the RC time constraints. Yet creative thinking combined with a positive attitude among senior uniformed Army leaders are the ingredients necessary if progress is to be made on these two important issues.

Second, ongoing efforts to make the Army and Air Force more mobile and rapidly deployable, similar to the sea services, need to be maintained at current tempo and maybe even accelerated. The Mobility Requirements Study validated the C–17 program, reaffirmed enhancement of the ready reserve force of transport ships, and called for 20 additional large roll-on, roll-off ships. This would allow the deployment of one light and two heavy Army divisions worldwide within 30 days. The formation of Air Force composite wings at Mountain Home Air Force Base (AFB), Idaho, and Pope AFB, North Carolina, is the Air Force solution to finding new ways to prepare its forces for rapid deployment. Such forces train together at home like they would fight when deployed overseas. The former, designated as an air intervention wing, includes bombers, fighters, tankers, and C[2] aircraft. The latter is considered a battlefield support wing and includes fighters, close air support aircraft, and tactical transports. It works closely with the Army's 82d Airborne Division at Fort Bragg, North Carolina.

Third, PME needs to be stressed even more during a time of diminishing resources, especially joint PME. There is a need for both field experience and education among military officers. Sir William Francis Butler, the noted 19th-century British soldier and author, said it well: "The nation that will insist upon drawing a broad line of demarcation between the fighting man and the thinking man is liable to find its fighting done by fools and its thinking done by cowards."[12] PME is central to the effort of maintaining a first-rate officer corps.

Lord Ernest Rutherford, British nuclear physicist and Nobel Peace Prize winner, was once quoted as saying, "We are short of money, so we must think." That is not a bad description of where the Armed Forces stand today. Education stimulates thinking. The challenge in these next few months and years will be not to cut education to such an extent that we actually find ourselves guilty of eating our own seed corn. Education, it must be remembered, is the foundation upon which the future is built. As Sir Francis Bacon noted, "Knowledge is power," and a strong military must have wise leaders who have not suffered because of excessive cuts in education.

Finally, I caution this generation of military officers not to be complacent about the next war. Success sometimes is seductive. The great victory won in the desert 2 years ago cannot be allowed to contribute to complacency in the years to come.

As a Nation, we emerged victorious from World War II in no small measure because of the moral and intellectual strengths at the highest levels of the American officer corps. Unfortunately, after World War II, we became complacent. Strategic thinking atrophied after 1945. In the nuclear age, many believed that the ideas and thoughts associated with classical military history and strategy had been rendered obsolete. Maurice Comte de Saxe, the famous French military analyst, noted that

> Few men occupy themselves in the higher problems of war. They pass their lives drilling troops and believe this is the only branch of the military art. When they arrive at the command of armies they are totally ignorant, and in default of knowing what should be done . . . they do what they know.[13]

Doing what one knows, rather than what should be done, is a problem that many military commanders have faced throughout history. It is a problem not unfamiliar to the American military in the recent past. I would contend that in Vietnam the American military did what it knew—fighting the conventional war that it had fought in World War II and Korea—rather than knowing what to do, fighting the revolutionary war in which it became engaged. It took 10 years to put together a strategy to win the war. By that time it was too late. The patience of the American public had come to an end.

The bitter experience of Vietnam, which resulted from a loss of strategic vision, sent American military men back to the study of war and military history. Students at the five command and staff colleges and the five war colleges are the beneficiaries of this renewed interest in the study of war. For some, there has been much to catch up on. For all, however, this educational opportunity has meant extensive reading, serious research, written analysis, seminar discussions, and old-fashioned thinking.

The U.S. military must not lose the ability to fight the big war. In light of the victory in the Persian Gulf War, I am reasonably confident that it will maintain this ability. At the same time, however, the U.S. military must devote more attention to the difficult problems posed by small wars—or to use the more current phrases, *low-intensity conflict* and *operations other than war*. Over our short history, we have had difficulty dealing with unconventional warfare—in the late 1800s fighting the Indians, early this century pacifying the Philippines, and most recently in Vietnam. Operations other than war will pose similar difficulties.

As I look close to our shores, at Peru, Colombia, Haiti, and the drug war, these are the kind of conflicts that will require more of our attention in the years to come. Such conflicts have a military dimension, but they are overwhelmingly political by nature. We have not understood this great truth on previous occasions when we have involved ourselves in such struggles. These will demand attention and efforts in the coming years.

We should have learned from history that wars—even major ones—can come about when least expected. The peace and tranquility of a European summer in 1914 was suddenly shattered by an assassin's bullet. The world was ill prepared for the tragic events that followed. We must maintain a ready, modern, and sufficiently powerful military that can meet any unexpected contingency.

We need to remind ourselves that, despite all the problems we have, America is the richest and most productive nation in the world today. No other nation comes close in terms of economic output, and none seems likely to overtake us for at least a generation, if then. We have both the ability and the resources to continue leading the free world. All we need is the will. Those who would pose a false choice between meeting our responsibilities abroad and meeting the needs of our people at home do our nation a disservice. For the truth is, we either meet both responsibilities or we shall meet neither.

In the post–Cold War era, leadership will not be easy. But the United States will have a leading role to play far into the 21st century. Now is the time to realize that taking the initiative is preferable to inaction, that leadership is preferable to self-doubt, that securing the gains democracy has made in the past decade is within our reach. We can do all this if we look upon the design of the future not as a threat but as a challenge.

Notes

[1] John M. Collins, "National Military Strategy, the DOD Base Force, and U.S. Unified Command Plan: An Assessment," Congressional Research Service report 92–493S (Washington, DC: Library of Congress Congressional Research Service, June 11, 1992).

[2] Colin L. Powell, "The Base Force: A Total Force," presentation to the Senate Appropriations Committee, Subcommittee on Defense, September 25, 1991; John M. Collins, "U.S. Military Force Reductions: Capabilities versus Requirements," Congressional Research Service report (Washington, DC: Library of Congress Congressional Research Service, January 8, 1992).

[3] Department of the Air Force, "The Air Force and U.S. National Security Policy: Global Reach—Global Power" (Washington, DC: Department of the Air Force, June 1990), 17.

[4] Department of the Navy, ". . . From the Sea: Preparing the Naval Service for the 21st Century" (Washington, DC: Department of the Navy, September 1992), 12.

[5] Ibid., 2.

[6] Colin L. Powell, "Report on the Roles, Missions, and Functions of the Armed Forces of the United States" (Washington, DC: Joint Chiefs of Staff, February 1993).

[7] Sam Nunn, "The Defense Department Must Thoroughly Overhaul the Services' Roles and Missions," *Congressional Record*, July 2, 1992.

[8] Colin L. Powell, testimony before the House Armed Services Committee, March 30, 1993, 10.

[9] William R. Manchester, *The Glory and the Dream: A Narrative History of America, 1932–1972* (Boston: Little, Brown and Company, 1974), 518–519.

[10] Ibid., 519.

[11] Les Aspin, remarks at the United States Air Force Senior Statesman Symposium, June 24, 1993.

[12] U.S. Congress, House Armed Services Committee Panel on Military Education, "Report of the Panel on Military Education," 101st Congress, April 21, 1989, 18.

[13] Ibid.

Chapter 3

Taking Stock of the New Joint Era

T he American military came out of Vietnam demoralized if not broken by the experience. The services all had serious problems, including racial friction and drug abuse. Toward the close of the conflict in Indochina, the Armed Forces instituted various far-reaching changes. Some of them were forced on the services, others were initiated from within the military. These changes included the end of conscription and the introduction of the All-Volunteer Force as well as the Total Force concept, plus a renewed emphasis on professional education for officers.

Decline and Rise

Change is never easy. The collapse of the Republic of Vietnam in April 1975 ended a long national nightmare. As the military sought to reconstitute itself from inside out, it also had to deal with a nation that wanted to turn away from things military. At the same time, the Armed Forces confronted continuing challenges posed by the Warsaw Pact while maintaining a substantial force structure but at the expense of readiness.

By 1980, however, defense spending was simply inadequate. The military had become a fundamentally hollow, unprepared force with ships that were unable to sail, aircraft that could not fly, weapons disabled by shortages of spare parts, personnel unsuited for service in the force, and inadequate operational training. The tragedy of *Desert One*, the unsuccessful attempt to rescue our hostages from Teheran that resulted in the death of eight marines, symbolized the state of disrepair to which the Armed Forces had been reduced in the post-Vietnam period.

When he entered office in 1981, President Ronald Reagan convinced Congress that defense cuts in the 1970s under Presidents Richard Nixon,

---

The original version of this chapter appeared in *Joint Force Quarterly* 3 (Winter 1993–1994).

Gerald Ford, and Jimmy Carter had left the Nation exposed. The humiliation of Iran holding Americans hostage for 444 days, along with the Soviet invasion of Afghanistan, convinced the public that change was required. Defense spending, which increased during the final years of the Carter administration, was raised substantially by the incoming Reagan administration.

Goldwater-Nichols

Early in the Reagan years, other changes affecting the military were also taking place. Two articles published in 1982—by General David Jones, Chairman of the Joint Chiefs, and by General Edward "Shy" Meyer, Army Chief of Staff—made the same point. The defense establishment was in need of substantial changes to improve the way it did business. So was born what came to be known as defense reorganization, which culminated 4 years later with passage of the Goldwater-Nichols Department of Defense Reorganization Act of 1986.

Goldwater-Nichols was fundamentally about rearranging power among institutions within the Department of Defense (DOD)—namely, the Chairman of the Joint Chiefs of Staff, the services, and the unified commands. It reduced the influence of the service chiefs and increased the power of the Chairman and commanders in chief (CINCs), the commanders with responsibility for employing U.S. forces in given theaters of combat.

It also helped simplify the chain of command. This occurred as a result of the 1983 House Armed Services Committee investigation of the bombing of the Marine barracks in Beirut. Among other problems, the committee found fault with a complicated chain of command. An example of how business was conducted before and after Goldwater-Nichols helps to illustrate this finding. The chain of command during the Vietnam war was anything but clear and simple. While Generals William C. Westmoreland and later Creighton W. Abrams ran the ground war in South Vietnam, the Navy ran its own air operations over the North, as did the Air Force. And while the Air Force ran tactical aircraft from headquarters in Vietnam, the Strategic Air Command maintained its own chain of command through the Joint Chiefs of Staff in Washington for B–52 missions against targets in the North. In other words, operational coordination was a nightmare. American military leaders violated one of the fundamental principles of war, unity of command.

Goldwater-Nichols corrected the problems of Vietnam by strengthening the authority of the theater commander. Thus, in the war in the Gulf, the Commander in Chief of Central Command, General Norman

Schwarzkopf, commanded all forces in the theater whether Army, Navy, Marine Corps, or Air Force. The military buzz word for this ability to fight together in a unified fashion is *jointness*. Unlike the experience in Vietnam, the effort was coordinated by a single commander in the theater running the entire show. Goldwater-Nichols made this unity of effort possible.

Professional Military Education

The House Armed Services Committee Panel on Professional Military Education (PME) was established in the wake of Goldwater-Nichols[1] and undertook the first comprehensive review of PME by Congress. Its charter was to assess the military's ability to develop strategists and to review joint education requirements under the Goldwater-Nichols legislation. The panel's findings appeared in a 206-page report that had two major thrusts. One established a conceptual model in which each level of schooling builds on previous levels and each college has a clear, fundamental teaching focus. The other urged resurrecting two joint colleges—the National War College (NWC) at the senior level and the Armed Forces Staff College (AFSC) at the intermediate level—to the prominence they enjoyed in the early post–World War II period. Under this scheme, schooling at service colleges would precede joint education.

The principal recommendations focused on joint institutions, a proposed National Center for Strategic Studies (as a reconstituted NWC was referred to) and AFSC. Numerous suggestions sought to strengthen these institutions by combining greater operational competence at the military level with sound, imaginative strategic thinking at the national level.

End of the Cold War

The Berlin Wall fell a few months after the House report on military education was issued, and, shortly after that, Secretary of Defense Dick Cheney and Chairman of the Joint Chiefs of Staff General Colin Powell crafted a new "national military strategy"[2] that envisioned the end of the Cold War. It differed from Cold War strategy in a number of ways. First, it envisioned the primary threat as regional rather than global. Second, it emphasized conventional forces instead of nuclear weapons. Third, forward presence replaced forward deployment as the key to protecting U.S. interests around the globe. The military would be primarily U.S.-based, especially the Army and the Air Force. Subsequently, the Base Force, articulated by the Defense Department, spelled out the new military strategy.[3] It envisioned a 25 percent reduction in both forces and funding by the mid-1990s.

Service and Joint Reorganization

In the midst of these momentous developments, each military department began efforts to reorganize for the future, as did DOD as a whole. The Air Force, for one, published a white paper entitled "Global Reach—Global Power" in 1990, a visionary document that outlined a strategic planning framework for the post–Cold War world.[4] Venerable institutions such as the Strategic Air Command, Tactical Air Command, and Military Airlift Command passed into history. In their place the Air Combat Command incorporated all winged firepower—fighter, bomber, reconnaissance, command and control, tactical airlift, and rescue—in one organization. The Air Mobility Command acquired most mobility and refueling assets: strategic transport, tanker, and medical evacuation aircraft. The number of major commands was reduced from 13 to 8.

The Navy—regarded as the service traditionally most resistant to change—also responded to the end of the Cold War and the Persian Gulf War in dramatic fashion by issuing a white paper in 1992, ". . . From the Sea."[5] The result of a year-long study, it incorporated two assumptions: America and its allies would control the seas, and most future military operations would be joint. This strategy symbolized a new way of thinking. The focus of future operations shifted from open seas to coastlines. In concert with the Marine Corps, the emphasis on littoral warfare marries naval forces and the priorities of both services. "The Navy and Marine Corps will now respond to crises and can provide the initial, 'enabling' capability for joint operations."[6]

In many respects, the Army instituted a number of far-reaching changes 20 years ago. The bitter outcome of Vietnam was reflected in three crucial decisions that affected this service more than any other: the end of the draft and beginning of the All-Volunteer Force, the creation of the Total Force concept, and the establishment of the Training and Doctrine Command (TRADOC) at Fort Monroe, Virginia. Recruiting high school graduates and adequately paying them built an Army of high-quality people. TRADOC yielded great dividends. First-rate training programs, as symbolized by the National Training Center at Fort Irwin in California, and a renewed emphasis on PME helped produce combat leaders who had studied war and were well prepared when called to action. Those officers responded magnificently in Panama and in the gulf with campaign plans that produced quick victories with few casualties. Although less prone to white papers than other services, the Army is indeed undergoing fundamental change as it becomes "A Strategic Force for the 21st Century." The Army is coming home; it will be primarily based in the United States rather than forward deployed as in the Cold War. Substantial force reductions have led to inactivating 4 divisions and 1 corps along with consolidating 51 war reserve stocks to 5.

As all the services reorganize for the post–Cold War era, each understands that most future operations will be joint or multiservice. This view was underscored in 1991 by Joint Publication 1, *Joint Warfare of the U.S. Armed Forces*. That document and the related effort to develop joint doctrinal publications will help the services to work more closely together in a period of declining budgets and force structure. Leading thinkers in each service can offer their creative talents toward integrating the disparate ways the military thinks about employing forces. The publication in 1993 of the first issue of *Joint Force Quarterly* was another tangible indication that jointness had finally come of age.

While the services were busy adjusting to the changed political circumstances in the world, the Chairman was also busy reviewing defense policy. As a result of the Goldwater-Nichols Act of 1986, General Powell issued a report on roles, missions, and functions of the services in 1993. Two considerations dominated the report: improving the way the Armed Forces fight, and saving money in the process.[7] The report noted the dramatic changes that have taken place already: the creation of Strategic Command, the elimination of nuclear weapons in the Army and the Marine Corps, and the end of the need to maintain chemical weapons brought about by the signing of the Chemical Weapons Convention in January 1993. The report also highlighted savings from further consolidation among the services of depot maintenance and flight training.

Testifying before the House Armed Services Committee in March 1993, General Powell, then Chairman of the Joint Chiefs, described the roles and missions report as "simply a snapshot of a continuous process of self-evaluation that occurs every day. The Joint Staff will continue to examine other areas for possible consolidation or elimination."[8] The Joint Staff will soon get more help. The DOD Authorization Act for Fiscal Year 1994 included a provision calling for the establishment of a commission on roles and missions of the Armed Forces. It will have seven members appointed by the Secretary of Defense and will issue a report within a year of its first meeting.

Jointness in the Post–Cold War Era

In September 1993, Secretary of Defense Les Aspin reported the results of the long-awaited *Bottom-Up Review*. The review envisions a force that is smaller than the Base Force, and appears to cost 10 percent less, designed to fight two major regional conflicts nearly simultaneously. Overall active duty strength will decline from 1.6 million to 1.4 million. The force level will allow for the permanent stationing of 100,000 military personnel in Europe and 98,000 in the Pacific. To bolster the capability of a smaller force, the Pentagon plans to add airlift and sealift, preposition Army equipment in both the Persian Gulf and Northeast Asia, develop and procure more precision guided weapons (especially antitank munitions), and improve Reserve component forces.

If truth be told, I have serious reservations about the *Bottom-Up Review*. Peacekeeping, peacemaking, peace enforcement, and other peacetime contingencies have increased dramatically in the brief period since the end of the Cold War. Such operations impinge on the military's ability to carry out the national military strategy to fight two major regional conflicts. In addition, I question that the force described in the review can fight two regional conflicts even if all U.S. involvement in peacekeeping operations was terminated; the overall force is too small. The *Bottom-Up* force is underfunded, overstretched, and verging on hollowness while a declining defense budget pays for nondefense functions such as industrial conversion, drug interdiction, and environmental cleanup.

As the size of the force decreases, so does our margin of error. As a result, the requirement for greater jointness increases as a way to compensate for smaller forces. This growth in jointness takes two forms: greater cooperation in the field and fleet among each service's respective combat forces, and greater attention to matters that concern two or more services in the planning, research, and development phases of the acquisition process. The former is the primary responsibility of the CINCs and the latter that of the Joint Chiefs working with the services. Airlift, prepositioning, sealift; command, control, communications, and intelligence; and space, ballistic missile defense, and advanced munitions are just some of the cross-cutting issues that must be addressed from a joint perspective early in planning and research and development.

Atlantic Command

The return of units formerly deployed overseas to bases in this country means that a larger and more important segment of the overall defense establishment will be stationed at home. Except for those forces attached to Pacific Command, all other forces in the United States now come under U.S. Atlantic Command (ACOM), which was established on October 1, 1993.

This was recommended in the Chairman's 1992 "Report on Roles, Missions, and Functions of Armed Forces of the United States" and is the fourth such effort. There was Strike Command in 1961, Readiness Command in 1971, and the Rapid Deployment Joint Task Force in 1980 (which is now Central Command). While service parochialism undermined the first two efforts, ACOM should succeed for two reasons: first, Goldwater-Nichols gave unified commanders authority over component commanders that they previously lacked, and, second, since 1986—especially after the Gulf War—jointness has not only become fashionable but has also proven itself.

Joint Exercises

Prominent among the activities of the trend toward greater jointness are training exercises. ACOM is charged with the joint training of forces based in the United States. Reductions in forces stationed abroad make it crucial that the forces that reinforce regional commanders arrive fully capable of operating as a joint team. The services had 5 months to prepare for the Gulf War, and we must assume that any potential opponent learned from that experience not to give the American military time to prepare for combat.

This is not an easy matter to work out. Service expertise comes first. Service personnel—both officer and enlisted alike—must first become skilled as soldiers, sailors, marines, and airmen. Service skills progress from the individual to the unit. Much time, effort, and training is needed to become combat ready, be it an infantry battalion, ship, or fighter squadron. Finding time for both service and joint training is difficult. Balancing service and joint needs may require emphasis on service training with field exercises and joint training with computer-aided staff exercises. Advanced simulation technologies now exist that allow service and joint staffs to participate in staff exercises from remote locations. This will result in improved joint interoperability.

There is still a requirement to conduct field exercises for forces that normally do not work together: Army armor units supporting Marine Corps infantry units, naval gunfire supporting Army forces, Air Force tankers refueling Navy fighters, Army helicopters working with Navy ships, and Navy attack aircraft providing close air support to Army and Marine Corps units. These are just some of the activities that require joint training exercises among the services.

At the same time, regional unified commands must also conduct joint training exercises in theater. And forces deployed from the United

States in the future will have to be well grounded in joint warfare fundamentals and better prepared to conduct combat operations on arrival in theater. If we fail to train in peacetime, we will have to learn in wartime at the high price of American lives.

Joint Doctrine, Training, and Education

Each service has come to understand the importance of doctrine, the prescribed procedures and fundamental principles for conducting combat operations. The Army established TRADOC 21 years ago. In 1993 the Navy and the Air Force established doctrine centers at Norfolk Naval Base and Langley Air Force Base, respectively.

As the importance of joint training increases in the post–Cold War era, so does that of joint doctrine. The newly established Joint Warfighting Center (JWC) will promote both joint doctrine and training. It consolidates activities of the Joint Warfare Center at Hurlburt Field, Florida, and the Joint Doctrine Center (JDC) already in Norfolk. Situated at Fort Monroe, Virginia, JWC is responsible to the Chairman through J–7 (Operational Plans and Interoperability). ACOM will also play an important role in evaluating, testing, and sequencing the development of joint doctrine by working closely with JWC.

Yet if current efforts to improve joint training and doctrine are to be institutionalized and have a permanent impact, more needs to be done. At present, JDC reviews recommendations for joint doctrine but does not formulate it. The time has come to increase the stature and responsibility of JDC by remaking it into a Joint Doctrine *Command* with a major role in formulating doctrine.

Careful consideration must also be given to where JWC is located in the Norfolk area. JDC is already there, as are TRADOC and the Naval Doctrine Command, ACOM, and AFSC, while the Air Force Doctrine Center is nearby at Langley Air Force Base.

The Chairman, Joint Chiefs of Staff, and the President of the National Defense University need to focus attention on the role of AFSC in this whole effort toward greater jointness. The purpose of the college is to prepare students for immediate assignment to the unified commands or to the Joint Staff. AFSC is intended to be a hands-on school, teaching students to cope with the kinds of problems faced in joint assignments. The absence of adequate wargaming facilities hinders AFSC in accomplishing its mission. Placing JWC at the college would resolve this inadequacy. At the same time,

AFSC offers JWC a source of expertise for evaluating and developing joint doctrine. Such a move would have a mutually reinforcing effect.

In 1923 Major George C. Marshall, the future Army Chief of Staff, described the regular cycle in the doing and undoing of measures for the national defense. He noted in a speech to the Military Schools and Colleges Association that "we start in the making of adequate provisions and then turn abruptly in the opposite direction and abolish what has just been done." Today, we are in the midst of making one of those changes in direction.

World conditions have changed. Both forces and defense budgets should be reduced. But President Clinton remarked at West Point in May 1993 that while "[defense] budget cuts . . . at the end of the Cold War were necessary . . . there is a limit beyond which we must not go."[9] He underscored that concern in an interview on the same occasion indicating that he wanted "to send a cautionary note to the House and Senate . . . that we have cut all we should right now."[10]

The challenge now is to reduce the size of our military without putting our national security at risk. There are still threats to American interests in the world that cannot be ignored. Military power still counts in the late 20th century and will in the 21st as well. The United States must maintain a ready, modern, and sufficiently powerful military to meet any contingency. As the military gets smaller, the necessity for the services to fight as an integrated force increases.

President Dwight D. Eisenhower got it right more than 30 years ago when he observed in a message to Congress that:

> Separate ground, sea, and air warfare is gone forever. If ever again we should be involved in war, we will fight in all elements, with all services, as one single concentrated effort. Peacetime preparation and organizational activity must conform to this fact.

Those thoughts of a former President and five-star general should guide both civilian and military leaders responsible for shaping the Armed Forces of today for the missions of tomorrow.

Notes

[1] Panel members included Joseph E. Brennan, George Darden, Jack Davis, Jon Kyl, Solomon P. Ortiz, Owen B. Pickett, John G. Rowland, and Ike Skelton (Chairman).

[2] John M. Collins, "National Military Strategy, the DOD Base Force, and U.S. Unified Command Plan: An Assessment," Congressional Research Service report 92–493S (Washington, DC: Library of Congress Congressional Research Service, June 11, 1992).

[3] Colin L. Powell, "The Base Force: A Total Force," presentation to the Senate Appropriations Committee, Subcommittee on Defense, September 25, 1991.

[4] Department of the Air Force, "The Air Force and U.S. National Security Policy: Global Reach—Global Power" (Washington, DC: Department of the Air Force, June 1990).

[5] Department of the Navy, ". . . From the Sea: Preparing the Naval Service for the 21st Century" (Washington, DC: Department of the Navy, September 1992), 12.

[6] Ibid., 2.

[7] Colin L. Powell, "Report on the Roles, Mission, and Functions of the Armed Forces of the United States" (Washington, DC: Joint Chiefs of Staff, February 1993).

[8] Colin L. Powell, statement before the House Armed Services Committee, February 1993, 10.

[9] Bill Clinton, remarks at the U.S. Military Academy commencement ceremony, New York (May 23, 1993), in *Weekly Compilation of Presidential Documents* 29, no. 22 (June 7, 1993), 997.

[10] *The Washington Times*, May 30, 1993, A6.

Chapter 4

Inspiring Soldiers to Do Better Than Their Best

Generally speaking, human beings have untapped reserves of courage and perseverance. Sooner or later, everyone taps these reserves when illness, death, or life's other trials and tribulations strike. But the pressures on warriors and military leaders are infinitely more demanding than on most individuals. To them, survival is incidental to mission accomplishment. Military leaders not only carry the burden of making competent military decisions in what Carl von Clausewitz described as the "fog of war," but they also must bear moral responsibility for their soldiers' lives. Commanders must carry intense physical and emotional burdens at the same time that they are trying to master their craft intellectually. Conducting war is a craft, not a science, because nothing is as intensely human or unpredictable. An analogy in civilian life is the physician who spends many years undergoing academic training and education but, in the end, is confronted with a living, breathing human being to heal, not a sterile laboratory experiment.

Most people possess a normal level of courage and resolution, which is further developed in soldiers through effective indoctrination accompanied by tough, rigorous physical and intellectual training. It is the military leader's task to capitalize on this training and lead soldiers past the normal point of human endurance and bravery systematically. Such leadership examples are more common than one might think; Nelson at Trafalgar, Napoleon at Austerlitz, Stonewall Jackson at Shenandoah, or Slim in Burma during World War II are just a few famous examples.

At the Line of Contact

Let us focus instead on several commanders in less well-known situations. In these circumstances, the intellectual leader's ability, exertion,

---

This chapter was previously published in *Military Review* (January–February 1996).

inspiration, or capacity to function under stress enabled soldiers to perform far beyond the point where a less-inspired commander would have taken them. Such leadership takes place at the immediate line of contact, where the fighting is the fiercest. It also takes place at intermediate levels of command, where the commander is very visible but is not necessarily wielding a sword, musket, rifle, or grenade launcher. Finally, it can be found at the overarching level of high command, where senior officers' vision, tone, or creativity often can lead to spectacular results in cases where more pedestrian leadership would accomplish far less. This chapter examines some examples of each to instruct and inspire.

The Civil War

At times, leadership on the firing line does not inspire men to use greater energy and dynamism, but rather restrains man's natural tendency to give way to fear under fire. Giving in to fear isolates the soldier mentally and erodes the organization as a cohesive unit.

Consider the Battle of Gettysburg, July 1–3, 1863, which allows us to focus on a "true man of iron"—Brigadier General Andrew A. Humphreys, 2[d] Division commander, III Corps, Army of the Potomac, on the pivotal day of battle.[1] During the battle's second day, Major General Daniel Sickles, III Corps commander, unwisely pushed his corps too far forward from the front lines of the Army of the Potomac. Sickles' order created a salient dangerously vulnerable to a Confederate Army flank attack. When the Confederate assault came, Humphreys was ordered to pull his 4,000-man division back nearly a mile, under fire, to avoid being totally isolated and destroyed. Under enormous pressure from both front and flanks, he executed this desperate task. On horseback (one horse was killed under him) and in full view of both his and the enemy's soldiers, he rode up and down the entire 1,000-yard division line, systematically ordering units to fire and then slowly retreat. Some units successfully executed this dangerous and complicated maneuver more than 20 times.

"Humphreys himself, according to one of his colonels, stayed at the most exposed positions in the extreme front, giving personal attention to all the movements of the division."[2] He had good brigade and regimental commanders under him, but action accounts clearly attest to Humphreys' personal control of the battle. He not only inspired his men to keep fighting, but by his calmness and control, he kept an orderly retreat from turning into a rout. In an hour, 1,500 of Humphreys' men were killed or wounded, but the division stayed intact and ready to fight when it completed its withdrawal.

Humphreys, a class of 1831 U.S. Military Academy graduate, was older than most of his peers. He was fiery of speech, a meticulous dresser, and exhibited a "personal fondness for battle." After the Gettysburg battle, he was assigned as General George G. Meade's chief of staff. While no doubt regretting the loss of his combat division, Humphreys brought the same personal attention to detail and control to Union Army staff operations as he did to 2ᵈ Division command. At war's end, he commanded II Corps, replacing the legendary Major General Winfield S. Hancock, who had suffered multiple wounds. Under Humphreys, II Corps never missed a step, enjoying leadership no less capable than Hancock's during the final 6 months of the war.[3]

World War II

Even in modern warfare, the presence of general officers at the right time and place can provide a spark plug for success. On June 9, 1944, 3 days after D–Day, then Major General Matthew B. Ridgway's 82ᵈ Airborne Division launched a frontal attack across a narrow causeway bridging the Merderet River in Normandy.[4] With no maneuver room, the attack stalled under intense German fire. U.S. vehicles and equipment blocked the causeway, and hundreds of U.S. paratroopers—dead, wounded, or paralyzed by fear and indecision—lay alongside the road.

"In the midst of this slaughter, Ridgway appeared on the causeway carrying his .30.06 rifle."[5] Ridgway, with his assistant division, regimental, and battalion commanders, reversed the flow of men away from the attack and across the causeway by exhortation, shouting, and physical coercion, but most of all, by example. Ridgway personally attached a towing cable to a disabled U.S. tank and, with the help of several soldiers, cleared a passage through the wreckage. Led by other senior officers, the airborne soldiers finally fought their way down the causeway and across the river.

Action accounts leave no doubt that Ridgway's personal example and intervention saved the day and enabled those present to do "better than their best." His presence and bearing, amid confusion and paralysis, is as good an example of courageous battlefield leadership as can be imagined. This command ability led him to World War II corps command, U.S. Eighth Army command, U.S. and United Nations (UN) Korean War forces' command and, finally, to assignment as the U.S. Army chief of staff.

The Korean War

UN forces, primarily American and South Korean, reached the Yalu River border between North Korea and China at two locations in late

November 1950, shortly before a massive and undetected Chinese communist force drove into the overextended UN front, inflicting one of the most disastrous defeats in U.S. military history. One advance to the Yalu was led by 21-year-old Army Second Lieutenant Robert C. Kingston, a K Company platoon leader, 3d Battalion, 32d Infantry Regiment, 7th Infantry Division.[6] On November 21, with his battalion thinly spread and isolated 32 miles south of the Yalu, Kingston was ordered to move 10 miles north to a small town. A small force of antiaircraft artillery (AAA) and machine guns, led by a first lieutenant, was added to Kingston's 33-man platoon. Because the AAA unit supported him, Kingston retained command, even though the AAA leader outranked him. In brutal weather, varying from 20 to 40 degrees below zero, this small force advanced as ordered. The next day, Kingston was ordered forward another 22 miles—his objective, the Yalu.

For 3 days, Kingston's force was unable to go the distance, due to terrain, weather, and communist resistance. By this time, Kingston's command included an engineer platoon, led by a first lieutenant; an artillery forward observer first lieutenant; a tactical air control captain; and a heavy mortar platoon, also led by a captain. The next day, a rifle company and artillery battery—both commanded by captains—reinforced "Task Force (TF) KINGSTON."

Although the rifle company commander at first "assumed command," it became quickly apparent that Kingston was in control. Within hours, the captain told Kingston to command and that he, the captain, would follow orders. By then, a major had also joined the task force, although his function remains unclear. Kingston's force fought forward, reached the Yalu and cleared a village on the riverbanks. Kingston himself neutralized a house controlled by five Chinese defenders.

Within 2 days, along with the entire UN force, TF KINGSTON was forced to retreat. All it left behind were a few lines in an official report and "the personal triumph of a 21-year-old second lieutenant." A combined arms force, which under normal circumstances would be commanded by a major or lieutenant colonel, had *crystallized* around the natural leadership of a young man who, by civilian standards, would have been considered too inexperienced for all but the most basic tasks. It is not surprising that Kingston retired as a full general after serving two Vietnam combat tours, working with the British Army Parachute Regiment in Malaya and serving as the first commander in chief, U.S. Army Central Command.

Vietnam

Sometimes, a battlefield leader can do so much that it is virtually impossible to encompass it all in a short narrative. Such was the case of U.S. Marine Corps Captain Jay R. Vargas, who commanded G Company, 2ᵈ Battalion, 4ᵗʰ Marines, 3ᵈ Marine Division, near the demilitarized zone in northern South Vietnam.[7] From April 30 to May 3, 1968, Vargas led his company in extraordinarily fierce combat against North Vietnamese troops in the vicinity of Dai Do village. He maneuvered his company under extremely heavy fire in offensive and defensive actions; personally led an assault on Dai Do, killing several enemy troops; and calmed a near-hysterical, less-experienced fellow company commander over the radio, which allowed his fellow commander to collect himself and resume effective command. While constantly under fire, Vargas personally resupplied his marines with ammunition. He was wounded three times but concealed his wounds to avoid evacuation.

Vargas, self-confident but without a touch of arrogance, was awarded the Congressional Medal of Honor for his actions. He provides a living example of a remark by former Marine infantry officer, now-retired Brigadier General Thomas V. Draude, that "the kindest and gentlest are also the bravest."[8]

Intermediate Command

Several historical examples follow, illustrating how active senior commanders, making decisions within range of enemy weapons, made the difference between complete victory and catastrophic defeat.

Waterloo

British Field Marshal Wellington's Waterloo command is particularly notable because he commanded a coalition, of which fewer than half the 68,000 soldiers were British. The other troops were primarily Dutch, Belgian, and German.[9]

The battle seesawed so frequently that only select examples of Wellington's on-the-spot command decisions can be provided. When Napoleon's French troops threatened to overwhelm the stone farmhouse at Hougoumont, Belgium, Wellington committed tactical reserves at the precise time to prevent the collapse of this crucial anchor to the allied right. A few hours later, when 18,000 French infantrymen came close to breaking the allied center, Wellington ordered two British infantry brigades forward to repel them. He personally directed British cavalry to charge the unbroken, advancing French infantry after the British "thin red line" had checked the initial French rush. Although it was dubious, even in 1815, to assume that cavalry could defeat infantry in good order, Wellington's calculation was correct—the French broke.

After this, it was the British and their allies' turn to hold against incessant French cavalry attacks.

> The French cavalry advancing in thick waves of regiments, some of which charged as many as 12 times that afternoon, boiled against and around the British squares, threatening the integrity of the line, which in places and at times was actually penetrated. Wellington was here, there, and everywhere. Occasionally, he popped into a square—the men opening ranks to let him in—and sat the charge out, uttering brief words of encouragement the while.[10]

In the last chapter of the battle, Napoleon's Imperial Guard—the never-defeated elite arm of the French army—attacked in one last spasmodic attempt to crush Wellington's exhausted troops. Wellington rode along the battle line to reposition troops and steel them for the onslaught. He ordered his leading units to open fire. Then, as the French recoiled from their last, failed attack, he ordered the allies to pursue the beaten French. The general assessment, 180 years later, is in accord with his own remark, made one day after the battle: "By God, I don't think it would have done if I had not been there!"[11]

The Civil War

Leadership at its best can result when a determined and morally courageous commander imposes his iron will on a battlefield where the issue is in doubt and the results are far from clear. On May 7, 1864, after 2 days of ferocious and indecisive fighting, Lieutenant General Ulysses S. Grant's Army of the Potomac faced General Robert E. Lee's Army of Northern Virginia in the Wilderness, just south of the Rappahannock River.[12] Union casualties during those 2 terrible days totalled almost 18,000; Confederate dead or wounded numbered roughly 12,000.[13] Neither side held a positional advantage over the other when the fighting died down.

Over 3 years, the Army of the Potomac had grown numb to lost victories caused by weak, indecisive, and inexperienced commanders. Examples of the Army's leadership problems include Brigadier General Irvin McDowell at First Manassas (1861); General George B. McClellan during the Seven Days (1862) and Antietam (1862); and Major General Joseph "Fighting Joe" Hooker at Chancellorsville (1863). Hooker gave in to his fears and led the Army of the Potomac back across the Rappahannock after being confounded and intimidated by Generals Thomas "Stonewall" Jackson and Lee. In May 1864, Union soldiers no doubt felt that the army would retreat as usual after being thrashed again by Lee's veterans.

Yet on the night of May 7, 1864, Grant's headquarters ordered the Army of the Potomac to move.[14] The direction was not immediately obvious to the rank and file. However, it would have been had they known that Grant had already informed President Abraham Lincoln that he intended to fight on the Wilderness line

> if it took all summer. . . . The road was crowded, and nobody could see much, but as the men trudged along it suddenly came to them that this march was different. Just then there was a crowding at the edge of the road, and mounted aides were ordering: 'Give way to the right!' and a little cavalcade came riding by at an easy jingling trot—and there, just recognizable, was Grant riding in the lead, his staff following him, heading south. . . . The Army had known dramatic moments of inspiration in the past—massed flags and many bugles and broad blue ranks spread out in the sunlight, with leadership bearing a drawn sword and riding a prancing horse, and it had been grand and stirring. Now there was nothing more than a bent shadow in the night, a stoop-shouldered man saying nothing to anyone, methodically making his way to the head of the column—and all of a moment the tired column came alive, and a wild cheer broke the night and men tossed their caps in the darkness. They had had their fill of desperate fighting, and this pitiless little man was leading them into nothing except more fighting, and probably there would be no end to it, but at least he was not leading them back in sullen acceptance of defeat, and somewhere, many miles ahead, there would be victory for those who lived to see it.[15]

When Grant skirted the Confederate lines and marched south, Lee had to follow to avoid being flanked and having his lines of communications cut. From that moment, the Army of Northern Virginia was on the strategic defensive, pressed remorselessly by Grant. Confederate Lieutenant General James Longstreet said of the Union leader, his West Point classmate, he "would fight [the Confederacy] every day and every hour to the end of the war." The Army of the Potomac won the Battle of the Wilderness because Grant refused to take counsel of his fears and uncertainties and commanded his forces accordingly.

High Command

There are few better illustrations of how a supreme commander's single-minded determination and professional competence can make a difference—regardless of separation from his fighting soldiers by distance—than the following examples from World War I.

History has not been kind to General (later Marshal) Joseph Joffre, the French army commander in chief during the first 2 years of World War I.[16] Conventional historiography has held that he was a dullard. Yet a close examination of Joffre's command of the 2-million-man French army during the first several weeks of World War I—August to early September 1914—demonstrates a tenacity, moral strength, and clarity of vision that look even better as time goes by.

As the German juggernaut drove through Belgium and northern France in August 1914 and the French army recoiled from its ill-conceived *Plan 17* offensives against the tactically and operationally superior Germans, Joffre remained imperturbable. His forces had been forced on the defensive, yet they had not been routed and, in most instances, had retreated in good order. Joffre assembled strategic reserves from the Alsace-Lorraine front, where the Germans had only conducted demonstration attacks. He moved these reserves to a line along the Marne River, just north of Paris, for a possible counterstroke. There, he ruthlessly sacked army, corps, and division commanders who failed to measure up under the super-human strain of keeping a retreat from turning into a total collapse.

At the same time, his German counterpart, Field Marshal Helmuth von Moltke, was suffering a crisis of confidence due to the stress of commanding the world's first modern industrial war:

> Thus the battle of France, absorbing the last energies of exhausted armies, was still smouldering slowly away without a decision on the battlefield. Perhaps the real, and ... the most dangerous competition was taking place in the two generals' headquarters, between Joffre, that huge, ruthless, self-confident, perhaps complacent man, and von Moltke, visibly prostrate with worry, with his almost hallucinatory awareness of all the moral and general issues at stake.[17]

> It mattered nothing now, in this crude business of leadership in war, that Joffre was an intellectual pigmy. Men trembled when his great nostrils flared and his eyes blazed with fury; and this engine that had kept the French going through catastrophe, was keeping them going

now. Equally it mattered nothing that von Moltke had a first-class intelligence and a brilliant staff record; he could no longer control his army because he had lost control of himself.[18]

When Joffre launched the French army and the small British Expeditionary Force in a counterstroke against the Germans in early September, the odds were still very even. The French had sustained hundreds of thousands of casualties—many more than the Germans—and were on the defensive everywhere. The Germans were equally exhausted from battle and pursuit but still retained the initiative. Yet when the French counterattacked, "an unjustifiable failure of nerve and resolution on the part of the German command," flowing more than anything else from von Moltke's inadequacies, led to a German withdrawal. Like Grant in 1864, Joffre refused to admit defeat and so drove his armies to victory.

A supreme theater of operations commander can also extract superior performance from his men and units through bold and innovative operational planning and forceful execution of such plans. This happened with British Field Marshal Sir Edmund Allenby's final offensive against the Turkish army in Palestine during September and October 1918, the last of a series of operational offensives that ultimately drove Turkey out of World War I.[19]

In the summer of 1918, British forces in Palestine possessed overwhelming superiority in infantry, horse cavalry (still very useful and effective as a mobile desert warfare arm), and artillery. Allenby's initial plan for a fall offensive against the Turks was conservative. In the plan, infantry divisions would penetrate the Turkish lines; then cavalry would pass through the gap leading to a comparatively short-range pursuit of the withdrawing Turks. A similar plan was proposed earlier by South African Lieutenant General Jans C. Smuts, representative of the British government and the Allied Supreme War Council, when he visited Allenby's headquarters in Palestine in early 1918.

However, by late August 1918, Allenby scrapped the conservative concept and developed a bold, decisive plan to strike against the Turks in Palestine. British forces would smash a deep, wide hole in the Turkish front with infantry divisions, then three cavalry divisions would be unleashed into a wide-ranging pursuit deep into the Turkish rear. The operational intent of this attack was to block almost all avenues of retreat for the Turks. It involved the cavalry breaking free of its supply trains and living off the land and demanded considerable powers of marching in extraordinarily hot weather by the entire force.

Beginning September 20, 1918, this bold scheme worked brilliantly—the Turkish front line was nearly annihilated. Three of Allenby's cavalry divisions began a pursuit that, in 5 weeks, took the British force nearly 350 miles from the vicinity of Jerusalem to Aleppo in southern Turkey. The cavalry sustained only 650 casualties and captured nearly 75,000 Ottoman prisoners. Allenby's British, Australian, and New Zealand troops rose to the occasion admirably. The British official campaign historian, writing later in a private capacity, said of the first, more conservative plan: "It was a sound enough scheme, but not a bold one, and it would have not led to the destruction of the Turkish armies."[20] In this case, the soldiers' best was beyond what they would have otherwise achieved due to the originality of their supreme commander's bold plan and his willingness to sacrifice security and take risks to maximize his advantages.

Inspiring Soldiers

Much can be said about battlefield leadership—based on these examples—that has enabled men to do "better than their best."

Professional Military Competence

Clearly, good leaders must be professionally competent in understanding the armed forces at their disposal and how to employ them best. But professional military competence is a matter of *character* as well as *intellectual ability*. One dimension of professional competence is that leaders must be able to do all this amid incredible moral, physical, and emotional pressure and nagging uncertainty. Doing well at employing combined arms on the exercise tables at the staff colleges is not enough. A good leader must take into account the raw realities of battle, such as lack of sleep, extreme temperatures, food shortages, disease, death, and imperfect knowledge of enemy strategies and conditions. This is where iron will, force of character, and self-confidence under stress play decisive roles. It also illustrates why the increasing sophistication of the U.S. military training centers and facilities, which can replicate at least some of these stresses during exercises, have done so much to improve the battle command and combat capability of our forces and their leaders.

Overcoming Fear

Leadership most often involves keeping men from doing what is natural as much as it involves inspiring them to superhuman feats. Fear is always present in battle, and most know their comrades are afraid. Upon reflection, they know their commanders are afraid too. But if soldiers see their commanders acting as if they know no fear and deciding with confidence what must be done, they will be motivated to stifle their own natural impulses toward fear and maximize their impulses toward acting courageously in the face of danger. In other words, good leaders:

- *lead by doing.* While those disposed to make decisions will sometimes be wrong, indecision in command is almost always fatal. All leaders cited in this chapter were intellectually active and never hesitated to make decisions and carry them out. They only changed a course of action when the situation demanded it.
- *take risks.* Some of these risks are physical and threaten the commander's own life and limb, as in most examples cited. Other risks are taken in a quiet office or a warm, dry bed, which may be more commodious than the average soldier's pack and bedroll.

Frequently, the risks taken by high commanders can impose much more terrible and exhausting strain than those taken by junior combat leaders. The former have thousands of lives in their hands; the latter, comparatively few. The weight of responsibility always falls on the man at the top—thus the familiar line of German Field Marshal Paul von Hindenburg about the 1914 Battle of Tannenberg, when the Imperial German army utterly defeated strong Russian forces. Hindenburg, who commanded the victorious German Eighth Army in the battle said, "I do not know who won the battle of Tannenberg, but I know who would have lost it."

So I return to my first point about willpower, endurance, and character. There is no reason to think the profession of arms attracts men and women any less intelligent than those who pursue any other field of endeavor. But intelligence, and the professional competence that it can generate, must be exercised in a maelstrom of stress, confusion, and emotion, for which there is no analogy anywhere else in human experience. When this happens, the leader who can clarify the situation through his own resolution and impose order on disorder by the sheer willpower of his actions will be the leader who can obtain "better than the best" from his soldiers. It is this margin of effort that can make the difference between victory and defeat on the battlefield.

Notes

[1] Most discussion of Brigadier General Humphreys is from Edwin B. Coddington, *The Gettysburg Campaign: A Study in Command*, 2ᵈ ed. (New York: Charles Scribner's Sons, 1964), 123–124, 411–424; and Harry W. Pfanz, *Gettysburg: The Second Day* (Chapel Hill, NC: University of North Carolina Press, 1967), 135–136, 347–380.

[2] Ibid., 413.

[3] Ezra J. Warner, *Generals in Blue: Lives of the Union Commanders* (Baton Rouge: University of Louisiana Press, 1964), 240–242.

[4] Clay Blair, *Ridgway's Paratroopers: The American Airborne in World War II* (New York: Quill Books, 1985), 266–279.

[5] Ibid., 275.

[6] Martin Blumenson, "Task Force Kingston," *Army* (April 1964), 50–60.

[7] Keith W. Nolan, *The Magnificent Bastards: The Joint Army-Marine Defense of Dong Ha, 1968* (Novato, CA: Presidio Press, 1994); William Weise, "Memories of Dai Do," *Marine Corps Gazette* (September 1987), 42–55; unpublished "Narrative Description of Gallant Conduct" prepared in support of Medal of Honor citation for Captain Jay Vargas, in Robert Goldich's possession; and personal discussion and observation of then Lieutenant Colonel Vargas when he and Goldich attended the same National War College class, 1981–1982.

[8] Remark made to the author sometime during 1991–1992.

[9] The literature on Waterloo is enormous. This section is based primarily on Elizabeth Longford, *Wellington: The Years of the Sword* (New York: Harper and Row, Co., 1969), 446–491; and David Howarth, "Waterloo: Wellington's Eye for the Ground," John Keegan, "Under Fire: Wellington at Waterloo," and Correlli Barnett, "Playing into His Hands: Bonaparte's Mistakes," in *Wellington Commander: The Iron Duke's Generalship*, ed. Pady Griffith (Strettington, UK: Antony Bird Publications Ltd., in association with the Wellington Museum, 1983), 91–138.

[10] Keegan, 122.

[11] Longford, 490.

[12] Bruce Catton, *A Stillness at Appomattox* (Garden City, NY: Doubleday, 1953), 90–92.

[13] R. Ernest Dupuy and Trevor N. Dupuy, *The Encyclopedia of Military History from 3500 B.C. to the Present* (New York: Harper and Row, Inc., 1970), 892.

[14] Catton, 91–92.

[15] Ibid.

[16] Correlli Barnett, *The Swordbearers: Supreme Command in the First World War* (New York: William Morrow and Co., Inc, 1964), 35–96; and Cyril Falls, *The Great War, 1914–1918* (New York: Capricorn Books, 1959), 37, 49–50, 63–73.

[17] Barnett, *The Swordbearers*, 85.

[18] Ibid.

[19] Cyril Falls, *Armageddon: 1918*, 2d ed. (Annapolis, MD: The Nautical and Aviation Publishing Company of America, 1979).

[20] Ibid., 35.

Chapter 5

The Constitutional Role of Congress: Lessons in Unpreparedness

ongress is responsible for ensuring the Armed Forces are prepared to preserve and protect the U.S. security. The key phrase in this statement is *Congress is responsible.* Under the Constitution, Article I, Section 8, it is the duty of Congress, not the President—let alone the secretary of defense or the joint chiefs of staff—to determine the size and composition of our Armed Forces. Article I, Section 8, assigns to Congress the power "To raise and support armies . . . provide and maintain a navy; [and] make rules for the government and regulation of the land and naval forces."[1]

Therefore, it falls to Congress to ensure our military strength is adequate to defend the Nation and national interests. Indeed, there is no more important duty for Congress than to provide for the common defense. We have a duty to our fellow citizens today and to future generations of Americans. We must not squander, through shortsightedness and neglect, the sacrifices that generations before us have made to secure the peace and security with which we are blessed. We must pass on the legacy of peace, prosperity, and freedom bequeathed to us. Congress, therefore, is ultimately responsible for approving a strategy to guide U.S. military policy and, above all, to establish a proper balance between national strategy and resources available.

Shaping Military Strategy

Historically, Congress has often failed in this responsibility. Since the end of the Cold War, many commentators have noted how badly the Nation has handled the aftermath of major 20th-century conflicts. Following

---

This chapter originally appeared in *Military Review* (July–August 1997) and was based on three speeches given by Rep. Skelton to the 105th Congress.

World Wars I and II, Korea, and again after Vietnam, we allowed military forces to deteriorate to a degree that cost us dearly in subsequent conflicts.

A speech made in 1923 by Army Major George C. Marshall decried a similar pattern of failure even earlier in our history. Marshall, of course, later became this century's most distinguished American soldier and statesman as Army chief of staff during World War II, secretary of state in the early Cold War years, and secretary of defense during the Korean conflict. "[F]rom the earliest days of this country," Marshall said "[the Regular Army] was materially increased in strength and drastically reduced with somewhat monotonous regularity."[2] Marshall felt it was perhaps understandable that there should be a reduction in the size of the military following a war, but the pattern was not quite so simple. Often, following a war, the Active Army size increased above what it had been before the conflict. Then within a few years—or even within a few months—it decreased below the prewar level. Marshall explained:

> It appears, that when the war was over every American's thoughts were centered on the tragedies involved in the lessons just learned.... So the Congress, strongly backed by public opinion, determined that we should be adequately prepared for the future, and accordingly enacted a law well devised for this express purpose. However, in a few months, the public mind ran away from the tragedies of the war and the reasons therefore and became obsessed with the magnitude of the public debt and the problem of its reduction. Forgetting almost immediately the bitter lesson of unpreparedness, they demanded and secured the reduction of the Army, which their representatives had so recently increased for very evident reasons.[3]

This pattern was seen at the turn of the century, after the Nation had just won a short, popular war against Spain. The pattern was repeated in 1917 where Marshall recalled seeing U.S. soldiers in France marching through the ice and snow "without shoes and with their feet wrapped in gunny-sacks"—Valley Forge all over again.[4] Yet in 1923, the public had already forgotten the lessons of that war and the cost of unpreparedness. Support for military expenditures quickly dissolved. Less than 20 years later, the United States was engaged in an even more destructive global war, for which we were, again, terribly unprepared.

Today, after the successful conclusion of the Cold War, we are well on our way to repeating the same mistake of denuding ourselves militarily. Today's world is no less turbulent or dangerous than it was during the Cold War. Regional threats, along with rising terrorism and the possibility of nuclear, biological, and chemical weapons proliferation, should cause us to keep up our guard.

What Is the Enemy?

I am frequently challenged by a question that has surely echoed before: "What is the enemy?" That question raises many others. Why continue to support more spending for defense when the Cold War is over? Why plan for two major regional contingencies (MRCs) when a second threat did not materialize during the Persian Gulf War? Why continue to pursue expensive new advanced weapons when U.S. technology was so dominant in Operation *Desert Storm* and when no other nation is spending nearly what we do on military hardware? Why keep a robust force structure and a fair-size personnel level?

There are no clear and simple answers. Indeed, there were no clear and simple answers in 1923. Any attempt to see into the future is like looking into a kaleidoscope. New patterns are constantly emerging; the only constant is that the colors will remain the same. In viewing the future of international affairs, we cannot foresee a "new world shape," but we know the colors are those of the human condition, including the character traits and circumstances that lead men to war. The need to prepare for conflict has not diminished merely because an era of conflict with a particular foe has ended and a new era, of yet uncertain pattern, has emerged.

"What is the enemy?" I must honestly say there is no precise answer. However, Congress will fail in its constitutional responsibilities if, once again, it allows the Armed Forces to become unprepared. In fact, for two reasons, a failure to support a strong military today would be even more unfortunate, and more unforgivable, than in the past. First, the United States is the only nation able to protect the peace. In the past, we were fortunate that our allies were able, often by the narrowest of margins, to hold the line while we belatedly prepared for war. Otto von Bismarck once said, "God protects fools and the United States."[5] Today, no one nation can prevent conflict from arising or respond decisively to a major threat. And, while I trust in God, I believe God has given us the tools we need to keep peace. It is our task to use them wisely.

Second, if we fail to maintain U.S. military power, the United States and, indeed, the entire world may lose an unprecedented opportunity to construct a lasting era of relative peace.

Our military strength is the foundation of a relatively secure international order in which small conflicts, though endemic and inevitable, will not decisively erode global stability. Our military strength is also a means of preventing the growth of one or more new powers that could, in time, constitute a threat to peace and evolve into the enemy we do not now foresee. Therefore, the additional investment required to maintain our military strength is disproportionately small compared to the ultimate benefits. Harry Truman stated this clearly: "We must be prepared to pay the price for peace or assuredly we will pay the price of war."[6] Truman's assessment is no less true now than when he first spoke those words.

These two premises—that the United States alone is able to protect the peace; and that adequate, visible U.S. military power may prevent new enemies from arising in the future—are the cornerstones of a sound strategy for the years to come. These are the premises I use to evaluate the current reassessment of defense policy.

The QDR Strategy

What are the Quadrennial Defense Review (QDR) strategy process and strengths, and how might they be improved? Although I will refer, at times, to a draft QDR statement of strategy recently printed by *Inside the Army*, it has not yet been officially released. Nonetheless, I refer to the draft because it reflects the thinking within the Pentagon to date and is a good start in defining military strategy for the future. However, I do not at all agree with the judgment, which appears to be emerging from the QDR, that the new strategy can be supported with a force smaller than the force determined to be necessary by the QDR's predecessor, Secretary of Defense Les Aspin's 1993 *Bottom-Up Review*.

The key theme of the new strategy includes three principal elements. First, U.S. military forces must be able to shape the international security environment in ways favorable to U.S. interests. This requires forward deployment of U.S. forces; various means of defense cooperation with allies, including security assistance; and joint training with allies and others. Second, we must be able to respond to the full spectrum of crises when it is in our interest to do so, which requires the ability to execute the full spectrum of military operations, including showing the flag to deter aggression; conducting multiple, concurrent, small-scale contingency operations; and fighting and winning major theater wars, including the ability to prevail in two nearly simultaneous MRCs. Third, the force needs to prepare now to meet the challenges of an uncertain future. This requires adequate size forces for air, sea, and land; increased investments in weapons modernization; robust efforts to exploit the evolving revolution in military affairs; and investments in research and development that hedge against the evolution of unexpected, but potentially dangerous, developments in future military technology.

Some say this strategy statement will fail because it is not selective enough in defining the challenges for which U.S. military forces should prepare. Some might complain that U.S. military forces are used too often in response to crises—such as Bosnia—that do not directly threaten U.S. security. I sometimes agree with those complaints. Others, with whom I do not agree, argue that the United States should give up the strategy of being prepared to prevail in two, nearly simultaneous MRCs—now called major theater wars—and instead prepare for one such conflict plus smaller peace operations. Still others say we should focus less effort on current challenges to our security and devote more attention to preparing for potential future threats from a peer or near-peer military competitor.

The QDR draft strategy statement is preferable to any of these alternative views. From a commitment standpoint, the emerging QDR strategy statement reflects that Presidents have long been able to commit large numbers of troops to sometimes long-lasting operations abroad pretty much as they see fit. President Bill Clinton has done so more than others, but he is not alone in asserting his authority as commander in chief to undertake major new missions abroad. Since Presidents can define which U.S. interests abroad are vital enough to require the commitment of U.S. forces, the military must be prepared to perform an extraordinarily broad range of operations short of war. It would be misleading, for military planning purposes, if a strategy statement identified only a narrow range of missions, when in fact the military can be called on at any time to carry out any imaginable mission while still preparing for major wars. Indeed, the key flaw of the *Bottom-Up Review* is that it fails to take account of the demands put on forces by missions other than the requirement to be prepared to fight two MRCs.

To give up the two-MRC requirement is a prescription for giving up our superpower status. If we lack the ability to respond to a second crisis after a first arises, in every case we would be hesitant in committing our forces to action in the first instance. Would we really respond to Saddam Hussein at the cost of critically weakening our deterrent posture in Korea? That is a choice we should never have to make.

For those who would spend less on maintaining current readiness in order to invest in future technology, I do not agree. Recent evidence reveals the post–Cold War world as more turbulent than ever. We must be prepared to deal with today's conflicts, or we may be critically weakened in confronting future challenges.

A new strategy statement that calls for forces able to shape, respond, and prepare would be a valuable contribution to the debate on U.S. military preparedness. It is a demanding strategy and, under current circumstances, one that will be challenging to fulfill. I am concerned that portions of the QDR are at odds with the requirements implied by the new strategy statement. Earlier this year, Secretary of Defense William Cohen assured the National Security Committee that the QDR process would be driven by strategy, *not* budget.

The new strategy, it seems, requires forces perhaps larger and certainly more flexible than the forces the *Bottom-Up Review* requires. The QDR strategy maintains the requirement to prepare for two major theater wars and recognizes the need to shape the environment, respond to lesser crises, and prepare for the future. Yet it calls for cuts in force structure. Indeed, the draft strategy statement suggests more reliance on Reserve component (RC) forces and our allies.

These are merely transparent excuses for making reductions in forces because of budget constraints, not strategy considerations. The bulk of RC forces are already built into war plans in a wholly integrated fashion, and other forces constitute a valuable strategic reserve. To depend on allies to carry out our strategy is the height of folly. Dependence on allies might force us to limit our strategic goals or make us hesitant to act. Also, it is not clear we can depend on allies to provide quality troops compatible with our own. We can and should expect allies to contribute in major conflicts—as they did during the Persian Gulf War—but we cannot afford to assume allied participation when making our own plans. The strategy emerging from the QDR is appropriately broad and demanding. The QDR, however, should address frankly which forces and what weapon investments are needed to execute it.

Congress must not repeat the mistakes of the past—mistakes that led to unpreparedness and battlefield disasters, such as the costly defeat at Kasserine Pass in North Africa during World War II and the destruction of Task Force SMITH during the Korean War. The price of unpreparedness is paid for in blood and lives of young Americans. If we let security erode, we may not have the strength to keep smaller-scale conflicts from weakening international stability. I also fear that major new threats will evolve that could have been prevented had we maintained our strength. Marshall's warning in 1923, though not heeded by his generation, should be heard by ours. Congress must not fail in its responsibilities.

QDR Budgetary Issues

Once again, as in the past, Congress appears unwilling to pay the price for peace. Since the mid-1980s, the Department of Defense (DOD) budget has declined by 40 percent in real, inflation-adjusted dollars. Weapons procurement funding has declined by 67 percent since 1985. We are now spending one-third as much on new weapons as we did in the mid-1980s. These reduced spending levels cannot continue without critically weakening our military capabilities. The proposed defense budget does not restore even modest growth rates in military spending. On the contrary, the administration's recently proposed budget plan projects that defense spending will continue down in fiscal year (FY) 1998.

The budget agreement announced in May allocates inadequate levels for defense across the board—both in budget authority and budget outlays. More important for long-term planning purposes, the QDR is being enacted on the assumption that defense budgets will be frozen at about $250 billion per year. Therefore, the military services must conduct planning on the assumption that any real growth in costs must be offset by reductions in other programs. Avoiding growth in costs is unlikely if we are to maintain a viable military.

The price of peace is small. The reluctance to support modest growth in defense spending is all the more tragic because it is so unnecessary. Looked at from a reasonable, long-term perspective, the price of peace today is extraordinarily small. In 1997, the defense budget was 3.4 percent of our gross domestic product (GDP). Under the new budget plan, by 2002, it will decline to 2.7 percent. As recently as 1986, defense spending was over 6 percent of GDP, and even at its lowest level in the mid-1970s, it was about 5 percent. Defense spending has declined to about 16 percent of the Federal budget share, down from 25 percent in the mid-1970s and 1980s, and down from 42 percent in 1970.

Real growth in defense spending is necessary to maintain a well-equipped, high-quality, well-trained force. Suppose we were to allow military spending to decline to 3 percent of GDP and then grow at no more than 1 or 2 percent in real terms each year thereafter. At this spending level, the defense budget would represent less than half the burden on the economy it did at the end of Cold War. This is a disproportionately small price to pay for the benefits we derive from having a force that can maintain a significant, visible U.S. military presence abroad, respond to crises across the spectrum of conflict, and still prepare for future advanced technological challenges.

However, instead of trying to bolster public and congressional support for so modest a defense burden, current leaders are trying to support its defense strategy with budgets that start out "two sizes too small" and that will become tighter and tighter as the years go by. As mentioned, DOD strategy articulated in the QDR is appropriately broad and demanding and is an improvement over the 1993 *Bottom-Up Review*. It recognizes that activities short of major theater war impose great strains on the current force structure. This must be taken into account in shaping future forces.

The civilian leadership in the Pentagon is mandating force reductions in the QDR to find savings with which to finance a modest increase in weapons modernization. Why this inconsistency? The QDR is actually being driven by budget, not strategy. Force cuts have to be considered because budgets cannot support existing force levels as well as increase funding for new weapons.

I would support budget-driven force cuts as a one-time deal. My concern, however, is that maintaining smaller forces with flat budgets will lead to perpetual budget shortfalls, cuts in weapon procurement programs, reductions in maintenance and training, and pressures to cut forces further. If current conditions continue, we will experience an erosion in our military capabilities until, with our forces no longer present in key regions of the globe, we must forego responding to important threats to the peace, which will encourage others to challenge us in strategic locations.

Need for Defense Budget Growth

It is ill advised for DOD to conduct planning based on flat budgets. Until recently, DOD insisted that modest growth was necessary in the long term. Former Secretary of Defense William Perry told the National Security Committee how DOD planned to reverse the decline in weapons procurement. Funding to "recapitalize" the force, he said, would come from three sources:

- The four rounds of military base closures, at considerable cost, would soon begin to achieve savings, and the entire increment would be used to boost procurement funding.
- Savings from acquisition reform, though not assumed in the budget, would also be allocated to procurement.

■ Modest growth in defense spending, then projected in administration plans, would also go for weapons modernization.

But how will we recapitalize the force now and in the future? How much can we count on saving from infrastructure reductions, outsourcing, inventory cuts, and other efficiencies to substitute for a growth in spending? Currently, DOD must reduce force levels in order to fund weapons procurement.

Historically, we have not been able to support a force of a given size with flat defense budgets. Recently, the Congressional Research Service did a study that measured the trend in defense spending relative to the force size from FY 1955, just after the Korean War, projected through the year 2000 under the administration plan. The study found that defense budgets have grown by about 1.7 percent per year in real, inflation-adjusted prices per active duty troop.

For defense budget analysts, this is not a surprising finding. For example, in the late 1970s, there was a debate over whether to increase defense spending by 3 percent per year. The premise was that defense budgets should increase in real terms over time for several reasons, one of which was to keep quality people in the force by providing a quality of life equal to that of the civilian sector. Also, the costs of modern, advanced weapon systems grow from one generation to the next. For instance, each generation of aircraft typically doubles in price, in real terms, compared with the previous generation. Although the services have always hoped that new weapons would be more reliable and cheaper to operate and maintain, this has never been the case. Since weapon systems are designed to maximize performance, operation and maintenance costs typically grow in real terms.

If DOD believes that the long-term cost of doing business has changed, it should explain why. A number of factors should make it more difficult to limit cost growth. For one thing, we have not been able to reduce the defense infrastructure size in proportion to cuts in the force size, and I am doubtful Congress will approve another round of base closures in the near future. That means we have to maintain a relatively large support structure, which drives up costs relative to the force size. We must also try to use technology to substitute for force size. Therefore, the capital investments required will be relatively large compared with the force size.

Moreover, with an all-volunteer force it is more important than ever to protect the quality of life. In recent years, we have skimped on military pay raises. Much military housing is in terrible condition, and we have only belatedly begun efforts to improve it. We have also deferred maintenance of military facilities for many years, and the backlog of requirements will inevitably catch up with us. Also, we have projected savings in military health care costs that will be extraordinarily difficult to achieve. Finally, requirements that the military comply with environmental regulations and with health and safety norms are increasing costs in every sector of society.

So the requirement to conduct planning on the basis of a flat budget is a prescription for perpetual underfunding of long-term defense requirements and the steady erosion of our military strength. Modest, steady, sustainable rates of real growth in military spending are necessary to maintain a well-equipped, well-trained, high-quality force large enough to carry out U.S. military strategy and protect U.S. national security interests.

Beware False Economies

For some, the notion that defense spending should grow over time seems alien. However, the notion that defense budgets should increase follows straightforwardly from clear thinking about defense. The only proper way to decide how much to spend on defense is to first decide on a military strategy that ensures national security. Then we must determine what size force we need to support that strategy. Finally, we must calculate what resources we need to ensure force quality.

Often, extraneous arguments about defense spending obscure this clear line of thinking. One common argument against defense spending is that today's potential enemies appear to spend less than the United States. The implication is either that threats are not so great as our planning assumes or that the U.S. military should be able to maintain its strength with much less money. The flaws in such reasoning are legion. For one thing, to maintain stability in their own regions, potential enemies must simply be strong in only one area of military capability. However, possible challenges to U.S. security interests come from so many different directions and in such a wide variety of forms that the United States must maintain strong military capabilities of all types. It must not be barely stronger than the Iraqs of the world.

Fundamentally, it is not enough for those who want to cut military spending to cite how much possible enemies spend. Instead, those who call for cuts should identify specific aspects of U.S. military strength they would give up. If they argue that North Korea is not as great a threat as U.S. military planners assume, then we should consider whether or not to weaken the U.S. military posture in Korea. Viewed from this perspective, the argument is harder to sustain. Despite whatever North Korea spends, our intelligence assessments tell us how threatening their military capabilities are. Anyone who looks closely at the situation is aware of how much damage North Korean forces could wreak even if confronted by strong U.S. and South Korean troops. Few, therefore, would want to encourage aggression by weakening our deterrent posture. So an argument based on North Korean or Iraqi or Iranian levels of military spending is irrelevant. The real issues: What are the threats, and what U.S. posture is needed to address them?

Another argument for cutting defense spending is that the United States is spending about as much today on defense in inflation-adjusted dollars as it did during the Cold War. The assumption is clear—with the Cold War over, we should be able to spend less. This argument is flawed. To maintain forces of a given size costs more over time because of the need to improve the quality of life, pursue advanced technology, and operate increasingly sophisticated weapons. The fact is that we have cut force size substantially since the Cold War's end. In 1987, the Active Duty force level was about 2.1 million. Today, it is about 1.4 million—about one-third less. A force this size understandably should cost more than a larger force did 25 or 30 years ago, but it is nonetheless substantially smaller and less costly than a force of the size that would be necessary if the Cold War had continued.

Four Guiding Principles

How should we think about defense spending? How much is enough for national defense? Two years ago, I prepared an alternative defense budget that I believed would be adequate to maintain U.S. military strength over the next 5 years. It calls for spending about $45 billion more on defense than the administration was projecting. I still think that an alternative budget is wise. In light of the new QDR, however, I want to discuss four guiding principles Congress should apply in deciding "how much is enough."

Maintain Force Levels

We should not cut force levels further. Reports that the QDR may include a decision to reduce total defense end-strength by as much as 144,000 individuals disturb me. Such reductions are destructive because they break faith with the men and women of the Armed Forces. Recent defense drawdowns have reduced total force levels by about one-third. This reduction imposes an immense burden on military personnel. People must change jobs more frequently to replace others who are leaving. Reduction imposes an immense strain on the military education and training system, and often people must begin new jobs without complete training. Reduction also makes the military personnel system brutally competitive. The pressure to force people out often means a single mistake can cost a good soldier his or her career.

Military planners call this "force turbulence." It has caused great turbulence in people's lives as well. I believe the Armed Forces have suffered this turbulence long enough. For years we have told them the problems would ease once reductions ended. We told them to "hang in there," that things would get better. It is not right to ask these people to go through another period of such turbulence.

For strategic reasons, we cannot afford to reduce force levels further. The services are being strained to the breaking point. They must perform multiple requirements imposed on them by the demands to be trained and ready for two major wars and to be actively engaged in the multiplicity of smaller operations that have proliferated since the Cold War ended. Already the Army is short 40,000 support position slots. This means that to conduct operations in Bosnia, support personnel must be taken out of continental U.S.–based units in order to fill out deploying units. The support personnel left behind must then do twice the work they should just to keep up. "Thinning" Army ranks further will inevitably make these shortfalls worse.

Increase Weapons Modernization Funding

We should increase weapons investments enough to get back to a steady-state replacement rate for major equipment items. Reportedly, a key QDR goal is to find funds to increase weapons procurement substantially. For several years, the target has been $60 billion a year. This requires a 33-percent increase above the $45 billion currently spent on procurement. I hope that the QDR will get there, though not at the cost of cuts in force size. I am doubtful, however, that $60 billion a year will be enough.

Currently, the Air Force and Navy have about 3,000 fighter aircraft in their inventories—2,000 in the Air Force and 1,000 in the Navy. If we assume a 20-year average service life for fighters—which is getting pretty long in the tooth—we must buy 150 aircraft a year to maintain a steady-state replacement rate. For the past few years, we have bought about 28 to 42 fighter aircraft per year. By my calculations, we must increase aircraft procurement by at least 400 percent to get to an adequate level.

The Navy needs a minimum of about 350 battle-force ships. If we assume an average service life of 35 years, we must buy 10 ships a year. Lately we have been buying four or five, so we need to double shipbuilding budgets to get back to a steady-state replacement rate.

Add to those increases the need to raise spending modestly each year to exploit new technology. What are we giving up by not modernizing as fast as we should, and how will we adjust to projected shortfalls? We may be able to keep some equipment going longer by pursuing upgrades instead of new systems. We may be able to limit cost growth between generations of new weapons by careful attention to cost, as reflected in the services' plan for the Joint Strike Fighter. All of these adjustments come at a price in reduced military strength. Compromises should be kept to a minimum.

Protect Military Readiness

We should not allow military readiness to decline. I am skeptical of DOD budget plans that show operation and maintenance costs declining in the future relative to force size. Base closures may produce some savings and better business practices, but it is unrealistic to expect training costs to decline or to plan on reduced maintenance costs for major weapon systems.

Improve DOD Business Practices

While improving DOD business practices can achieve some savings, I am skeptical about claims that we can achieve large savings. It may be true there is waste in defense business practices, but waste is not a line item in the budget that we can easily eliminate. I am concerned that proponents of revolutionary changes in government procurement practices are vastly overstating the achievable savings.

These four principles—maintaining force levels, increasing weapons modernization funding, protecting military readiness, and not overstating savings from improved business practices—force me to conclude that currently projected defense spending levels are not enough. If defense spending is not frozen at current levels, we will see the erosion of U.S. military strength and, as a direct result, the slow decline of U.S. global leadership.

QDR People Issues

The men and women who serve in our Armed Forces, and the civilians who support them, are the most important resource the Nation has in protecting its security. An ambitious strategy accompanied by inadequate resources places tremendous strain on these people. It is easy to lose focus when resources are tight. The money Congress provides for defense, the weapons the services buy, the logistics infrastructure undergirding the force, the military doctrine strategists pronounce, the campaign plans commanders devise—everything comes down to the soldier at the "point of the spear." Therefore, our Armed Forces men and women deserve sufficient materiel and moral support to allow them to do what we ask of them. In peacetime, however, we often forget the costs of war and neglect to pay the price of peace.

In assessing how we treat our people, I am torn between two strong feelings: I am concerned that the pressures put on servicemembers and DOD civilians are growing to the breaking point; and I do not want to discourage those who are willing to serve from joining the Armed Forces or from staying in. On the contrary, I hope to encourage those who are willing and able to serve their country.

The fact that we are now at peace and no single enemy threatens us does not mean military service is any less necessary or any less valued than in the past. The burden of maintaining peace lies on the shoulders of those who serve, and it is no less critical a mission than any soldier, sailor, marine, or airman has ever had before. The bottom line is we need the dedicated, patriotic people defense requires.

Focus on People

One of the things that most impressed me about former Secretary of Defense Perry was his focus on people. When he became defense secretary, he went to military bases around the world to talk with service people. "Management by walking around," he called it. A direct result of his walking around was renewed emphasis on improving quality of life.

For us who knew him to be a hardware expert, his focus on people was greatly welcomed. The value of his focus on people was the message he sent to the troops. It was noticed throughout the military and did much to prevent an unbridgeable rift between the administration's civilian leaders and the men and women in uniform. The example he set is one we in policy-making positions should take to heart. The U.S. military is a complex human culture. We must always consider its human dimension in making choices on strategy, budgets, programs, social rules and regulations, or any other aspect of policy.

I believe it was a mistake that the QDR did not include a separate panel on people. The QDR comprised six panels: strategy, force structure, modernization, readiness, infrastructure, and intelligence. An integration panel linked it all together.

So many of the issues the QDR addresses come down to people. For example, what stresses and strains does strategy put on people, given the force structure available to implement it? How does quality of life in the military affect mission readiness? How does military training, education, and leadership development affect the military ability to exploit new technology effectively? How will reductions in the defense infrastructure affect morale? All QDR panels touched on people issues to some extent—but did not address many critically important people issues. Do military people understand how their jobs contribute to the common defense? How do the changes in society as a whole affect the military—changes that include increasing opportunities for women, growing proportions of two-income households, sexual harassment problems, and race-relations dynamics? Is there, as many fear, a growing gap between military culture and civilian society, and how will this affect public support for national security and the willingness of future generations of Americans to serve?

The answers to these questions have as much to do with national security as the budget size or the quality of new weapons technology. If the pressures on our Armed Forces do not ease, the military may begin to lose many of its best and brightest people. Those I have talked to often cite three reasons why good people leave the force: the operations tempo (OPTEMPO) is too high; they have concerns about their families; and they are uncertain about the future.

Stretched and Stressed—High OPTEMPO

A most pressing issue is how current demands on the force are affecting troops. Two years ago, Lieutenant General Theodore Stroup, Army deputy chief of staff for personnel, was asked what it was like for soldiers who served in an Army that was then composed of 520,000 active duty personnel. Soldiers, he said, were "stretched and stressed" by the demands being put on them. When asked what the effect would be when the number dropped to 495,000 as was then planned, he answered, "stretched and stressed all the more."

Recently, DOD has proposed reducing the Army size to 475,000, which the Army resists. Meanwhile, actual strength has eroded to about 490,000, even though the official end-strength target required by current law remains at 495,000. It is widely reported that the QDR will reduce Army end strength by 15,000 or more. So Army people will be "stretched and stressed all the more." At what point does all this stretching and stressing reach the breaking point?

Each of the services faces the same issues. Recently, a senior Navy official testified before the National Security Committee about the difficulty the Navy has had keeping forces on station as much as it had planned. In large part, this is because the Navy, to its credit, rigidly tries to limit overseas deployments to 6 months and puts other constraints on the amount of time units may be away from home. In the same testimony, however, the official defended the decision to reduce the Navy end strength by 11,000 in order to find money for equipment maintenance. The two issues cannot be separated—as end strength declines, we can either increase personnel deployment times, or we can reduce deployments, which means we cannot fully support military strategy.

For those of us who frequently talk to people in uniform, this message comes across loudly. Last Thanksgiving, in Hungary, I visited soldiers from Missouri and asked each of them how many military deployments they had been involved in during current enlistment periods. Several had two deployments, a few had three, and one sergeant had five.

Every time I visit the troops, I hear similar stories. I am convinced that current measures do not adequately identify the extent of the problem. Even in the Navy, the pace of deployments for individual sailors is not directly measured and limited. And in the other services, there is no systematic way to measure the extent of individual deployments, so we really do not know how much stress we are putting on individuals.

Another thing the QDR does not address is how to measure the strain put on individuals in the uniformed services and a means of controlling it. I recently saw a draft list from the Air Force of some things we should be measuring. It poses numerous questions, including the number of:

- people who have temporary duty assignments of less than 90 days a year; 90 to 120 days; over 120 days a year. If too many people deploy on a constant basis, that is a sure sign of an excessive OPTEMPO.
- people who work 40 to 45 hours per week; 45 to 55; over 55. Some jobs require long hours, but if the trend over the whole force is up, that is a major stressor.
- aircraft crews that receive waivers of training-hour requirements. If the trend is up, too many people are doing too many other things than their primary jobs.
- major exercises people are engaged in, on average, per year.
- people who are delayed in meeting training qualification requirements for position upgrades.

- enlisted personnel who are pursuing college degrees, and how many officers are pursuing advanced degrees. How many of each fail to complete course work? A decline in the number of people pursuing advanced education is a good measure of stress on the force.
- people who have accrued leave exceeding 60 days.
- fathers who have missed a child's birth due to a temporary duty (TDY) assignment. How many have been assigned TDY within 30 days of a child's birth?

The list is extensive. I am convinced measures such as these show a dramatic increase in all of the services' OPTEMPO. Unless we can manage the degree of strain put on the force and do something to control it, we will have real trouble in retaining good people.

What are the causes of such apparent problems? To me, the root cause is a tendency to underestimate requirements for military operations while still preparing adequately for full-scale war. In the past, the military services worried less about the impact of small-scale military operations because the force was relatively large, so a small deployment was not felt. Smaller military operations were also relatively rare. That is the main reason why current measures of stress on the force are inadequate.

Now the force is smaller, and military operations have become more frequent and of longer duration. One calculation in this year's *Army Posture Statement* is striking. Over the 40 years from 1950 to 1989, the Army was engaged in 10 deployments. In the 7 years between 1990 and 1996, the Army was engaged in 25 deployments. Meanwhile, the Army's size declined by one-third and the budget dropped by 39 percent.

Aspin's 1993 *Bottom-Up Review* did not come to grips with the impact of a larger number of operations on a smaller force. The *Review* simply assumed a force designed to fight two MRCs would be large and diverse enough to handle any number of smaller operations. Only now are the services beginning to understand why this Cold War thinking will not do. For each Army unit deployed in an ongoing operation, four units are needed in the force: one unit deploys; another prepares to deploy; a third is coming off deployment; and a fourth is depleted because some of its troops were drawn on to fill out a deployed or deploying unit.

Also, only a part of the Army is available for deployments due to education and skills training requirements, in transit, or in support functions and other troop positions. According to the General Accounting Office, 63 percent of Active Duty Army troops are deployable at a given time. So, out of the 495,000 total, 312,000 troops are available for operations. By December, 1996, 35,800 Army troops were deployed, mostly to Bosnia. This does not count the number of troops forward-deployed in Korea. Multiply 35,800 by 4, and the number of troops affected by deployments is 143,200, which is 46 percent of the deployable force. The other 54 percent of the force is supposed to be training hard to be ready to fight two major theater wars.

This is why I am concerned about the impact of further reductions in Army force levels. At any one time, a large part of the Army is either involved in operations or is directly affected by them. Now the plan is to reduce further the overall number of personnel without reducing the number of divisions or missions. If the reductions come from division strengths, some specialties will have even lower manning levels. I do not believe DOD adequately understands the strains that further reductions will put on the force.

So how can we resolve these problems? Each service has been searching for ways to manage resources to meet the needs, but how successful are the solutions or, if successful for the present, how viable will they be in the future? One solution has been to use RC volunteers to fill out deployed units. A key issue here is, when will we reach the limit of Reserve availability? Reservists willing and able to volunteer have come forward already for one duty tour in either Haiti or Bosnia. There may not be enough volunteers available in the future, and involuntary RC mobilization would soon cause many Reservists to quit. Also, RC mobilization is expensive. Reservists receive full pay and benefits once activated. Congress continues to offset supplemental funding for military operations with rescissions, forcing costs to be absorbed within the overall defense budget.

Another potential solution may be to reduce nondivision support troop levels in order to fill out division slots, but too often we lose sight of the fact that support personnel perform assignments critical to mission effectiveness. Intelligence collection, for example, is a support function, yet operations cannot proceed without adequate, timely, and usable intelligence. Nor can operations proceed without supplies, medical care, or any other basic services that support activities provide.

Military Families

The second reason for personnel leaving the services is concern for their families. Today's all-volunteer force is quite different from past draft armies. People who choose the military as a career make up a larger share of the force. This is a positive trend; sophisticated weapon systems require highly trained professionals. Our Armed Forces set the standard to which other nations aspire.

As a whole, troops are older than in the past. Today, 64 percent of Active Army personnel are married, and except for the Marine Corps, the proportion is similar in the other services. The modern U.S. military cannot maintain its high quality without adequately taking care of military families—"We enlist soldiers, we reenlist families."

In the early days of the all-volunteer force, we did not adequately care for families. Military pay levels eroded. Military housing and other facilities were in awful condition. Social problems that plagued the rest of society—including drug use and racial tensions—also affected the military.

Since then, attention to needs has improved dramatically. Pay raises in 1979 and 1980, and more attention to family needs, have been tremendously beneficial. The military has led the way in responding to social problems.

However, I am fully aware of continued shortcomings. Strains on military families are growing, and we are not doing as good a job as we should in protecting them. Many of the strains, of course, are inherent in the nature of military life. Military personnel are necessarily away from home for extended periods of time. Military families move frequently, making it difficult for spouses to build careers, which itself strains marriages. It is all the more important, then, that we devote special care and attention to military families.

The most important correction needed is to limit OPTEMPO so military personnel are not away from their families for longer periods than necessary. It is especially important that TDY be kept within limits. We also need to ensure that military pay keeps up with civilian sector pay.

In addition, we must preserve some of the benefits military families rely on. I am disturbed by proposals to eliminate commissaries and exchanges. Also, because of the military's demands, it is critically important to assist military families in having access to quality child care. We must also protect quality health care. Military families care deeply about education for their children, and we need to ensure the availability of the highest quality education. One of the most important initiatives DOD has undertaken recently is improving housing. While some housing is very good, much of it is not. I have seen housing with broken appliances, cracked walls, warped floors, peeling tile, inadequate heat, and stopped-up drains—with very poor responsiveness from maintenance staffs. This must change; we have to do it as quickly and efficiently as possible. The QDR will suffer from a major gap if it does not address the military family quality of life.

Uncertainty and Turbulence

A third reason people leave the force is uncertainty about the future. Many military people tolerate the stresses placed on them because they believe things will get better. If things do not get better, the best people could throw in the towel and leave.

There has already been a defense drawdown that reduced active component force levels by about one-third. This drawdown imposed immense burdens on military personnel. People had to move to new jobs much more frequently because of the need to replace the large number of people leaving the service. The drawdown imposed a strain on the military education and training system and has made the military personnel system brutally competitive.

These factors directly affect people's abilities to meet career goals. Officers cannot count on receiving the education they need to advance. The amount of time officers spend in command assignments—where they can learn their trade—has declined significantly. Officers once had 2 years of previous command experience at lower levels before rising to battalion command. Now they have 12 to 18 months. As a result, our officers are not adequately seasoned, which sets them up for potential failure.

These changes, together with a high OPTEMPO, create much uncertainty about the future. Unless we stabilize the force, pay adequate attention to training and education, and allow good people to progress through the ranks in a predictable manner, the best people will not remain in the force.

Already, good people are leaving. It would be wrong to attribute the exodus to external factors. For example, many say pilots are leaving in large numbers because airlines are hiring again. That may be a factor, but not the main one. The best people in the services will always be confident of opportunities in the civilian sector. Those we want most to keep in the force are precisely the people who can always find lucrative careers on the outside. The issue, then, is not what lures people away, but what drives them to leave. Good people do not sign up for the military as a career because they expect to make a lot of money—they need enough to provide security for their families, but they are not going to be lured away simply by higher salaries. Good people leave either because military service no longer offers them the rewards they expected or because the burdens of service have become too great.

Civil-Military Relations

There are other people issues the QDR should address. One is the broad issue of civil-military relations. The issue has many aspects. There is a widening cultural rift between those in the military and the civilian society they serve.

We ask a great deal of the people in uniform. Sometimes, we may expect too much. Failures in military conduct seen in sexual harassment allegations at Aberdeen Proving Grounds, Maryland, or in the Tailhook episode reflect a cultural gap that will continue to widen unless all parties are careful in their judgments. When such issues arise, some military personnel react by criticizing civilian society for imposing too much on the Armed Forces. "Outsiders" conclude that military culture itself is flawed. In my opinion, both are wrong. Yes, I think there are failures within the military, but I also believe the military can be counted on to identify and correct its failures. No, I do not think the military can be exempted from advancing social norms—including requirements for sexual and racial equality. I also recognize that the military is not identical to civilian society. Congress has a special responsibility to take care of the military personnel from whom we ask so much. It is incumbent on us to close the gap between military and civilian society before it grows into a gulf.

In this chapter I have called attention to the fact that Congress has often failed in its responsibility to provide for the common defense and that I fear we are again embarked on a course that will leave our forces ill-prepared for future challenges. I have also argued that a failure to maintain military strength will encourage the evolution of new international threats that otherwise would not arise to challenge U.S. security.

This is a strong, but sincere, message. It is one many will find difficult to accept. I have tried to make my point carefully, explain my reasoning, and use good facts and figures to support my conclusions. Sometimes, however, an argument needs something stronger. This reminds me of a passage in General Douglas MacArthur's autobiography *Reminiscences* in which he discusses a meeting he had with President Franklin D. Roosevelt in the mid-1930s. MacArthur was then Army chief of staff, and he and Secretary of War George Dern were making an appeal to the President for more defense spending. Secretary Dern, wrote MacArthur, quietly explained the deteriorating international situation and appealed to the President not to economize on the military. Roosevelt was unmoved and reacted to Dern with biting sarcasm. Then MacArthur joined the argument, which became more and more heated. MacArthur explained that

In my emotional exhaustion, I spoke recklessly and said something to the general effect that when we lost the next war, and an American boy, lying in the mud with an enemy bayonet through his belly and an enemy foot on his dying throat, spat out his last curse, I wanted the name not to be MacArthur, but Roosevelt. The President grew livid. 'You must not talk that way to the President!' he roared. He was, of course, right, and I knew it almost before the words had left my mouth. I said I was sorry and apologized. But I felt my Army career was at an end. I told him he had my resignation as chief of staff. As I reached the door his voice came with that cool detachment which so reflected his extraordinary self-control. 'Don't be foolish, Douglas; you and the budget must get together on this. . . .' Neither the President nor I ever spoke of the meeting, but from that time on he was on our side.[7]

I hope this Congress will not require an appeal like MacArthur's to remember the lessons of the past—that the price of unpreparedness is paid in war. The price of peace is much less. Therefore, let us treasure the Americans who wear our country's uniform—let us appreciate them, encourage them, but most of all, let us take care of them. After all, it is they who bear the burdens of defending America's most precious virtue—freedom.

Notes

[1] United States Constitution, Article I, Section 8.

[2] George C. Marshall, address to Military Schools and College Association, March 1923. The speech originally appeared in "Factors Contributing to Morale and Esprit de Corps," by General L.R. Gignilliant in 1923.

[3] Ibid.

[4] Ibid.

[5] Quotation is attributed to Otto von Bismarck.

[6] This quotation has been popularized over the years and is attributed to Harry S. Truman. Truman actually said, "We can well afford to pay the price of peace. Our only alternate is to pay the terrible cost of war." *Quote* Magazine, August 5, 1951.

[7] General Douglas MacArthur, *Reminiscences* (New York: McGraw-Hill, 1965), 101.

Chapter 6

Intelligence Support of Military Operations

S ome have described the 20th century as an epoch of total war for the American people. The assertion has considerable justification. Two world wars and the conflicts in Korea, Vietnam, and the Persian Gulf have marked decisive points in our history. In addition to hot wars, we have seen the peaceful conclusion of the Cold War, which required a massive investment in defense and the establishment of large military forces.

Combined, these conflicts—hot and cold—resulted in millions of deaths, countless injuries, endless destruction, warped economies, disrupted families, and other misery. Yet the Nation and its allies survived. The Armed Forces have redeemed the Wilsonian ideal of making the world safe for democracy. Taking a long view, America and its allies did not for the most part go to war in vain. U.S. security interests have been protected and American ideals have set a global standard even in countries that fail to live up to them. American shortcomings are real, but they pale in contrast with those of powers that have met with defeat—Nazi Germany, Imperial Japan, the Soviet Union, and Saddam Hussein's Iraq.

Given the decisive impact of war in this century, no one should be foolish enough to resort to combat unless it is unavoidable. Even the young have seen enough—via television if in no other form—to know about limited war. Most believe, however, that to avoid war or avert defeat should war break out, we must be prepared to fight effectively.

We cannot predict the nature of warfare in the next century. But we do know that we must prepare for an array of new contingencies. Technology is changing so rapidly that some observers refer to an emerging military technical revolution. Many regard capabilities based around air-launched precision-guided munitions (PGMs) and information systems as

---

This chapter is based on an article published in the spring 1998 issue of *Joint Force Quarterly*.

key to the American way of warfare in the coming decades. PGMs were used with considerable effect in the Gulf War and have become a focus of strategic planning. Although expensive and not a panacea, they can do extensive damage and minimize the loss of noncombatant lives.

Precision munitions, however, require reliable information: good intelligence. PGMs must be targeted exactly. The urgent need for precise intelligence to conduct operations—information superiority—underscores the need to grasp the evolution of military intelligence. Notwithstanding public fascination with covert operations mounted by the Central Intelligence Agency, most of the Nation's intelligence effort is concentrated in the Department of Defense. Aside from bureaucratic distinctions between the national and the tactical level, intelligence support has become increasingly important for military operations in the post–Cold War world.

Because of its growing importance and the absence of debate on the subject, it is useful to review the course of military intelligence from a peripheral concern of headquarters staffs to an integral component of every combatant command down to the lowest tactical echelon. That evolution reflects, in particular, the close relationship between intelligence capabilities and the effectiveness of aerial bombardment.

The Two World Wars

The intelligence arms of the Army and Navy date back to the last century, and Air Force intelligence was part of that service since its inception in 1947. Much of the early intelligence work by the services focused on gathering basic intelligence—order of battle, terrain, ports, and foreign defense industries. It came from reports by attachés whose major qualification for assignment abroad was an independent income. Except during World War I, much of the military intelligence effort could charitably be described as superficial. Even the excellent analysis done by a handful of cryptographers did not prevent the Japanese attack on Pearl Harbor.

But intelligence did not initially occupy a significant role in one particular military technical revolution earlier in this century. Following the lead of the Italian airpower theorist Giulio Douhet, military aviators sought victory by attacking enemy industrial and political centers. These assaults aimed at destroying the economy of a sophisticated nation without defeating its forces in the field. But airmen did not seriously analyze the nature and location of key enemy facilities. Photographic surveillance was often an orphan; the emphasis was on acquiring and training to use bombers.

Airpower came of age in World War II, but its accomplishments did not completely validate the strategy favored by its supporters. Despite the emergence of independent air forces, advocates of strategic bombing never demonstrated that it alone could defeat an enemy. It was not precision attacks against German factories and transportation centers that characterized the initial stages of the air campaign in Europe, but massive nighttime area bombardment designed to break enemy morale. It proved frustrating to hit targets with sufficient precision to knock out industries for significant periods. Without adequate fighter protection (especially early in the war), navigational capabilities, and intelligence data, the bombing of Germany was largely directed at its urban population centers. Later, when air superiority was achieved, daylight precision bombing of key targets contributed to the Normandy invasion and the drive into Germany; but it did not preclude bloody ground fighting. Moreover, postwar analyses of Allied bombing suggested that its effects were often inflated.

The success of bombing was limited by both aircraft and bombsight capabilities as well as German opposition, but the availability of intelligence was also a critical factor. It was difficult to take usable photographs at night, and reconnaissance by day was hazardous. Analysis of pressure points in the enemy economy took time. Damage assessments were largely casual and inaccurate. Intelligence analysts and operators were often at loggerheads on bombing results.

The bombing campaign against Japan presented a somewhat different challenge. Although its economy was highly developed, the Japanese industrial base was generally not concentrated in large, easily identifiable complexes but in small factories or homes. Intelligence clearly indicated that Japan was preparing to counter a possible American landing on its home territory with massive ground forces that would inflict horrendous U.S. casualties. Thus there was a persuasive case for area bombardment, and it was undertaken in 1945 with ruthless efficiency against tinderbox cities such as Tokyo, Osaka, and Kobe. The campaign reached a climax with atomic bomb attacks on Hiroshima and Nagasaki. Although Japan had been weakened by military defeats and a highly effective economic blockade, airstrikes, especially the atomic bombs, hastened the end of the war. Civilian losses from both conventional and atomic attacks were enormous.

Despite the limitations of air campaigns, there were advances in military intelligence during World War II, including photographic reconnaissance based on the work of George Goddard and other pioneers who adapted specially designed cameras for aircraft use. Careful analysis was done by civilian experts brought into the Office of Strategic Services to identify targets vital to German and Japanese war efforts. Combined American and British experts achieved great cryptographic successes, setting a pattern for postwar collaboration.

The Cold War

The defense establishment was reorganized after World War II. The National Security Act of 1947 created the post of secretary of defense, a separate Air Force, and the Central Intelligence Agency to coordinate all-source analysis and human intelligence collection. The late 1940s brought fiscal austerity, and military intelligence atrophied along with other defense capabilities.

As part of the buildup in the wake of the Korean War, military intelligence agencies began to grow and acquire the organizational structure that would make them major components of the Cold War military. New and specialized agencies would emerge to deal with cryptography, photographic interpretation, and satellites; and an Intelligence Community was organized under the Director of Central Intelligence to ensure collaboration and prevent expensive duplication of effort.

Much defense planning was based on increasing nuclear capabilities. These weapons made it possible to design air campaigns that could realistically destroy an enemy industrial base along with virtually everything else. The logic of nuclear warfare as it evolved, however, did not lead to a widespread acceptance of its practical utility. Once nuclear parity was reached, decisionmakers perceived that the use of nuclear weapons was inherently a worst case scenario and that, short of direct threats to the national survival, their military usefulness was strictly limited.

During the Cold War the Intelligence Community necessarily focused on the Soviet Union together with the Warsaw Pact countries and Communist China. Concern over the military capabilities and intentions of the communist world, especially after a nuclear strike on American territory became possible, led to the growth and technological sophistication of U.S. intelligence. The requirement for accurate information on a secretive Soviet Union led to overflights by manned aircraft (in the wake of the shootdown of a U–2 in 1960) and the development of satellites that could peer into the deep recesses of communist territory with increasing discrimination beginning in the early 1960s. It became possible to calculate accurately the number of Moscow's intercontinental missiles and launch platforms and assess Warsaw Pact intentions regarding the North Atlantic

Treaty Organization (NATO). Moreover, the Intelligence Community provided information for arms control agreements and defense planning.

The key recipients of intelligence were Washington decisionmakers— the White House, the secretaries of state and defense, and the joint chiefs of staff. Decision cycles were lengthy, and there was opportunity for exhaustive studies and voluminous national intelligence estimates.

Given the danger of nuclear war, intelligence support of military forces engaged in limited wars, even in Southeast Asia, was largely a byproduct of assets designed for superpower targets. Satellites might be redirected for a time, reconnaissance aircraft assigned to tactical missions, and signals from Third World countries exploited; but the emphasis—and the organization and methods of intelligence agencies—remained on the Soviet threat.

Bombing campaigns during the Korean and Vietnam conflicts failed to accomplish all (or even most) of what their proponents predicted. For various reasons it was deemed unwise in both wars to attack the sources of industrial production since they were outside the theaters of operations— in the Soviet Union or China. The primary effort was on interdiction and tactical support to combat units. The outbreak of the Korean War required a frantic effort to rebuild surveillance systems to enable allied forces to target North Korean facilities. While air superiority and the destruction of the few strategic targets were accomplished early in the war, the effort to interdict enemy supplies and reinforcements was limited by inadequate targeting data and weaponry. Although airpower contributed significantly, it did not isolate the battlefield, and the war dragged on for 3 years.

There was enormous debate during the Vietnam conflict over a bombing campaign known as *Rolling Thunder*. Target selection by political leaders in Washington and political constraints on American strategy hampered prosecution of the war. All sides were concerned that sophisticated and expensive aircraft were being used on minor targets such as individual trucks and small troop concentrations. But locating targets was difficult. Aerial surveillance was hindered by triple canopy jungle, and the effects of ground sensors were mixed. The extent to which interdiction actually reduced communist infiltration was widely disputed. Today, most observers concede that the costly air campaign did not accomplish its goals, at least until targets in Hanoi were struck in 1972.

The Armed Forces went through a difficult downsizing and readjustment in the years after Vietnam, but those years also saw the start of a technological shift resulting from improvements in electronics and communications. These advances, most related to computerization, were not at the time widely seen as changing the nature of operations. The focus of military planning remained on the threat posed by a Soviet Union whose decline was not immediately apparent.

Since the mid-1980s, some of the most notable technological advances have occurred in the field of military intelligence, including lasers, cameras, radars, sensors, miniature television links, e-mail, networked computers, and new forms of communications equipment.

After the Cold War

The collapse of the Soviet Union revolutionized the geopolitical environment in which the Intelligence Community operates. Although nuclear forces in the former Soviet Union must not be overlooked, most observers believe the United States is likely to face challenges far different from those of the Cold War. That means intelligence agencies that long focused on the Soviet Union must now provide real-time tactical intelligence on places such as Somalia, Cambodia, Bosnia, and Iraq. This requires new collection and communications systems as well as organizational flexibility that does not come easily to any bureaucracy. Yet there are interesting continuities between intelligence today and that of the pre–Cold War era. Technological advances make it possible to accomplish missions once considered impractical.

The Iraqi invasion of Kuwait in 1990 was countered by a coalition led by the United States. The dramatic victory in *Desert Shield/Desert Storm* reflected not only the changed nature of war but the emergence of advanced and arguably revolutionary military technology. Capabilities developed during the Cold War, especially laser-guided PGMs, proved particularly useful against Iraqi forces even though extensive adaptation and jury-rigging were necessary. It was possible to identify and attack military (chiefly air defense), industrial, and communications facilities, largely by crippling combat capabilities. The enemy was blinded by a precision air attack on its command centers, but there was no direct attack on the Iraqi population. Air defense networks were destroyed, columns of tanks were identified and reduced to scrap metal, and Iraqi aircraft fled to Iran for safety. The air campaign helped ensure that enemy resistance to the ground campaign was vastly weakened and allied casualties were light. Despite media claims, airpower alone did not achieve victory; the ground campaign was necessary to drive Iraqi troops out of Kuwait.

For television viewers far from the battlefield, dramatic footage caught laser-guided PGMs delivered exactly on target, occasionally entering specified windows. Leaving aside the possibility that the military released only the best coverage and the fact that PGMs were just a fraction of the ordnance used, precisely striking targets demonstrated that the capabilities propounded by airpower pioneers decades ago were realized on the battlefield. PGMs are costly and wars will still be fought "on the ground and in the mud," as General George C. Marshall commented, but these weapons are nevertheless a major part of future warfare.

Looking Ahead

PGMs depend on precise intelligence. For a bomb to enter a window, detailed information is needed on the use and configuration of the building. Obtaining it is not simple or inexpensive. While satellites, manned reconnaissance aircraft, and unmanned aerial vehicles (UAVs) may offer excellent overhead photography, not all targets are above ground. In addition, photography may not yield information on the interior. Other disciplines are necessary, including signals intelligence and human intelligence. Analysts must combine disparate data from all collection sources and give it to the decisionmaker within a definite timeframe. Hard decisions have to be made regarding priorities; mapping the entire Earth would be prohibitive even for the world's only superpower.

In a military technical revolution, innovations in weapons and equipment lead to new doctrine and organizations. Decades passed before the Air Force became a separate service. Even then, many military leaders and civilian strategists failed to integrate airpower fully into planning and operations. Today, new intelligence technologies, organizational structures, and the knowledge and skill to exploit them are being introduced simultaneously. A phenomenon of *Desert Storm* was the way in which informal liaison among various echelons and stateside components supplemented formal command patterns. This situation was especially noticeable when hard-pressed intelligence officers in the Persian Gulf region established direct links to Washington-level analysts by e-mail or secure telephone.

The Gulf War was a decisive victory that provided a host of lessons. Leaving aside the absence of good intelligence on Saddam Hussein's intentions before his invasion of Kuwait, there were unacceptable delays in transmitting data and aligning various computer links. Reams of paper were hand-carried within the theater because of inadequate transmission capabilities. The accuracy of bomb damage assessments (BDA) was controversial. The nature and extent of Iraq's chemical weapons capabilities and programs were a mystery until long after the end of hostilities.

Congress and the Pentagon carefully studied the effectiveness of intelligence during *Desert Storm* and incorporated its lessons into subsequent operations, especially Bosnia. Interoperability and the connectivity of communications capabilities reportedly are greatly expanded. Procedures for BDA have been examined. Efforts have been made to bring diverse elements of the Intelligence Community together to support commanders, and better links have been forged with the intelligence activities of foreign militaries. But anomalies exist. Decades after Goddard's work in configuring aircraft with special camera systems, naval aviators in combat jets have used handheld cameras to photograph ground installations in Bosnia.

Mastering the lessons learned during *Desert Storm* as well as the infrastructure established to support U.S. and NATO forces in Bosnia are only initial steps toward integrating intelligence into the post–Cold War defense establishment. Concepts such as dominant battlefield awareness, information superiority, and full dimensional protection may not adequately describe how forces will fight, but they are evolving in both Congress and the Pentagon. By all accounts, the military of the future will demand more effective information and intelligence. This is a necessity unless one plans to fight with obsolete technology, larger numbers of troops, and more civilian casualties.

Careful employment of advanced weaponry based on sophisticated intelligence can permit attacks on military assets, decisionmaking headquarters, and communications networks without the area bombing of cities that characterized World War II and was envisioned in the nuclear strikes of the Cold War. They can launch planes or missiles against vital targets, not jungle trails or empty buildings. But there are unavoidable costs. Increased intelligence may absorb a greater portion of the defense budget. In the sprawling Intelligence Community, there are undoubtedly cases of waste and duplication. At the same time, increased investments in advanced intelligence technologies are clearly in the national interest.

Chapter 7

International Engagement: Why We Need to Stay the Course

A decade ago, events took place in Europe and the Soviet Union that, for the United States, were the beginning of the end of a long struggle—a struggle that was characterized by terrible sacrifices in Korea and Vietnam; by periods of great national confidence and occasional episodes of uncertainty; by debates in the halls of Congress that were sometimes historic and solemn and sometimes partisan and shrill; and, above all, by a widely shared sense of national purpose that endured despite occasionally bitter internal divisions.

The constancy with which the United States carried out its global responsibilities over the long course of the Cold War is a great testimony to the character of the American people and to the quality of the leaders who guided the Nation through often trying times. In spite of the costs, in the face of great uncertainties and despite grave distractions, our nation showed the ability to persevere. In doing so, we answered the great question that Winston Churchill once famously posed: "Will America stay the course?"[1] The answer is, we did.

Today, we need to raise a similar question once again, but this time for ourselves and in a somewhat different form. Today, the key question is perhaps more challenging because it is more open-ended. It is, "Will we stay engaged?"

Engagement, while not yet widely embraced as a characterization of our basic global posture, seems to express quite well what we need to be about today—that we need to be engaged in the world and that we need to

---

This chapter was previously published in *Military Review* (March–April 1999).

be engaged with other nations in building and maintaining a stable international security system.

Engagement will not be easy to sustain. Indeed, as has become clear in recent years, it will be as challenging to the United States to remain fully engaged today as it was to stay the course during the Cold War for the following reasons:

- We face challenges to our security that in some ways are more daunting than those we faced during the Cold War.
- It will often be difficult to reach domestic agreement on foreign affairs because legitimate, deeply held values will often be hard to reconcile.
- We will have to risk grave dangers and pay a price to carry out our responsibilities, and because of the costs, it will sometimes be tempting to think that we would be more secure if we were more insulated from turmoil abroad.
- We will have to struggle mightily not to allow domestic travails to divert us from the vigilance that we must consistently pursue.

But our political system, which encourages open debate and constantly challenges leaders to rise to the demands of the times, gives us the opportunity, if we are thoughtful and serious about our responsibilities, to see where our interests lie and to pursue our values effectively. While engagement in the world may sometimes be difficult to sustain, it is nonetheless necessary. Moreover, it has succeeded in bolstering our security.

Engagement Is Difficult

Engagement is difficult, first of all, because it entails costs and carries risks. In an age of chemical, biological, and nuclear weapons of mass destruction, the United States faces particularly grave dangers. To quail in the face of these risks would be far more damaging to our security than to confront them—but we should not underestimate the dangers we face. Engagement is also difficult because it requires us to make policy choices in which values we hold dear are troubling to reconcile. Constructive engagement with China, for example, requires that we reconcile our deeply held convictions about human rights abuses with our knowledge that a policy of isolating China would be self-defeating.

Engagement with long-standing allies may also be turbulent at times. Many, if not most, of our allies have not, for example, wholeheartedly supported our efforts to enforce sanctions on nations that we believe are guilty of sponsoring international terrorism or that we see as threats to global peace.

A related difficulty of engagement is what might be called the paradox of burdensharing—getting allies to do more often requires that we do more as well. We will sometimes become embroiled in undertakings overseas that, at face value, cost us more than our immediate interests appear to justify. The obvious example is Bosnia. The reason we must, nonetheless, be engaged is that our overarching interest in building effective security cooperation with our allies requires that we exercise leadership.

Engagement is also difficult for domestic political reasons. To be blunt, no one gets elected by promising to devote a great deal of time and attention to foreign affairs. Those in positions of responsibility must make compromises, choose between alternatives that are often "bad" and "less bad," take risks to get things done, and bear the criticism if initiatives fail.

Finally, engagement is difficult because it is financially expensive. In recent years, it has been difficult to find the resources to meet obvious needs in defense and foreign affairs because of pressures to reduce the budget deficit. Now that the deficit has been brought under control, a part of the discussion of budget priorities ought to be how to restore a reasonable level of investment in meeting our international security requirements.

Engagement Is Necessary

Despite these difficulties, there is no alternative to continued, active U.S. engagement in the world. We persevered in the Cold War precisely because we felt it was our responsibility as a nation to defend against tyranny. In the name of that moral mission, we may sometimes have asked too much of ourselves, and particularly of our sons and daughters in the military—but it was nonetheless a goal worthy of the American people.

Now we have a very different moral responsibility before us that is equally important. Our responsibility now is to use our unchallenged position of global leadership in a fashion that will make the universal hope for peace, prosperity, and freedom the norm of international behavior. If the United States were not to try, at least, to use its current position of strength to help construct an era of relative peace and stability, it would be a moral failure of historic magnitude. More than that, to fail to exercise our strength in a fashion that builds global cooperation would also, in the long run, leave us weaker and more vulnerable to dangers from abroad.

We need to be engaged because only the United States can provide the leadership necessary to respond to global and regional challenges to stability, and only the United States can foster the growth of regional security structures that will prevent future challenges from arising. Likewise, we need to be engaged because our continued presence gives other nations confidence in our power and reliability and makes us the ally of choice if and when conflict arises. We also need to be engaged because only by actively shaping effective regional security systems can we create an environment in which nations that might otherwise challenge stability will instead perceive a community of interests with the United States and with our regional allies. Additionally, we need to be engaged because only by recognizing and responding to the security concerns of other nations can we expect them to support our security interests and concerns. Cooperation from other nations is essential to deter and defeat enemies who want to undermine global order.

Not everyone agrees on the necessity for engagement. Some traditional champions of a strong national defense argue that engagement puts too much emphasis on peacekeeping or humanitarian missions, which are costly and not directly related to the overriding responsibility of U.S. military forces—to prepare for major conflicts.

For others, who believe the world ought to be more peaceful and less militarized since the Cold War ended, engagement seems to emphasize security matters at the expense of other interests, including human rights, fair trade practices, and environmental protection. Some even see engagement as a questionable rationale for continued high military spending in a world with no direct, obvious U.S. threats.

Proponents of a strong national defense should reconsider their position in view of the compelling evidence that engagement is essential to our military security. Similarly, those who believe that conflicts can be prevented by promoting multilateral cooperation should understand that military engagement abroad is essential to build and enforce a more peaceful, cooperative world order in which our other interests and values can flourish.

Two points must be made:

- Smaller-scale operations demand more resources than military planners had assumed. The answer is not to foreswear such operations, but rather to acknowledge the resource demands and meet those requirements.
- It is important to be selective in making commitments and in using the military. Above all, we need to ensure a balance between the interests we have at stake and the commitments we are making.

Effective international engagement requires much more active and extensive U.S. military involvement abroad than many expected. In the wake of the Cold War, we decided to maintain a permanent military presence of about 100,000 troops in both Europe and Asia. These deployments, in retrospect, hardly appear excessive. On the contrary, our forces in Europe, if anything, have been badly overworked. They have been involved in countless joint exercises with old and new allies and with former enemies that have been critically important in building a new, cooperative security order in Europe.

Engagement has also entailed a constant, rotational presence in the Persian Gulf—a commitment which, we now should recognize, is on a par with the commitments we have maintained in Europe and the Far East. It has involved military intervention in Haiti, an ongoing peacekeeping operation in Bosnia, and literally dozens of smaller-scale military operations. One thing should be clear: as long as we are actively engaged abroad, the pace of military operations is likely to be much more demanding than anyone had imagined a few years ago.

We in the Congress must keep this in mind when it comes to resourcing the military. Engagement costs money. This policy cannot be pursued cheaply. We need a strong, well-resourced military to execute this strategy.

Engagement Has Succeeded

Perhaps the most important thing we need to keep in mind is that the U.S. policy of engagement has been a success. Yes, we have suffered some failures. No, we have not accomplished everything we might have hoped. Yes, we have made some mistakes. But failures, shortcomings, and mistakes are inevitable in international affairs—there has never been a government in history that has not run into such difficulties.

Engagement is as centrally important to our security—and to the prospects for peace in the world—as containment was during the Cold War. Perhaps above all, the key issue is whether we will persist despite the fact that the struggle to maintain relative international peace will never be concluded. This is not a struggle we can see through to the end. It is, nonetheless, an effort that we as a nation must continue to make.

Note

[1] Winston Churchill, as quoted in Stewart Alsop, *Stay of Execution: A Sort of Memoir* (Philadelphia: Lippincott, 1973).

Chapter 8

Whispers of Warriors:
The Importance of History
to the Military Professional

W hen I was a boy, every now and then my father would let me wear his sailor's hat. It was a very special keepsake, navy blue, embroidered in gold thread, with the name of the ship he so proudly served, USS *Missouri*, boldly emblazoned on the front. It was always a special occasion for me to wear that hat. When I wore it, I felt an unusual connection to my father and the men with whom he served during World War I. It was as if whispers of warriors floated inside that hat—whispers of important lessons learned through experience in battles past.

Perhaps spurred by stories from my father and keepsakes such as his hat, I have maintained an abiding interest in the military and military history. In my capacity as the ranking Democrat on the House Armed Services Committee in Congress, I work very closely with the military. Congress has a constitutional duty to raise and support armies and to provide and maintain a navy. It is a grave responsibility. While authorizing and appropriating funds for the engines of war are important military roles of Congress, ensuring our soldiers, sailors, marines, and airmen are mentally prepared for the exigencies of war is a greater one. Congress must work with the Armed Forces to ensure the strategic flame burns bright, that the next generation of military leaders is capable and ready to assume the mantle of generalship in the tradition of General George C. Marshall and Admiral Chester W. Nimitz.

When diplomacy fails, the fates of nations rest in the minds and hands of their militaries. Paradoxically, the most grave course of action a nation can undertake must be accomplished by a group unable to practice regularly its profession. Sir William Francis Butler, the noted 19ᵗʰ-century

This chapter was originally published in *Naval War College Review* (Summer 2000).

British soldier and author, said that "the nation that will insist on drawing a broad demarcation between the fighting man and the thinking man is liable to find its fighting done by fools and its thinking done by cowards." While armies, navies, and air forces can train, conduct exercises and war games, and shoot ordnance on instrumented ranges, for obvious reasons they cannot fight in the name of preparedness.

Why Study History?

All the great commanders have benefited from a strong foundation in military history. Consider the words of a few of the masters of war:

Military history, accompanied by sound criticism, is indeed the true school of war.

—Henri Jomini

The study of military history lies at the foundation of all sound military conclusions and practice.

—Alfred Thayer Mahan

[History is] the most effective means of teaching war during peace.

—Helmuth von Moltke ("the Elder")

The science of strategy is only to be acquired by experience and by studying the campaigns of the great captains. Gustavus Adolphus, Turenne, and Frederick, as well as Alexander, Hannibal, and Caesar, have all acted upon the same principles.

—Napoleon Bonaparte

Only the study of history is capable of giving those who have no experience of their own a clear picture of what I have just called the friction of the whole machine.

—Carl von Clausewitz

When giants of warfare—the likes of Jomini, Mahan, the elder von Moltke, Napoleon, and Clausewitz—agree universally on the importance of history to the military officer, one must take notice.

Their message is clear. Through the study of history, military officers can gain a semblance of experience in the art of war, even in the absence of fighting. Within the written histories of battles and wars spanning three millennia reside the experiences of the best and worst to practice the military arts in combat. Through history, the whispers of our forefathers are brought to life. They tell the tales of great nations, how they rose, and why they fell. They share secrets of war, from the painful, gut-wrenching decisions of commanders ordering men into harm's way, to the less frenetic and more rarefied analysis of grand strategy. They provide guidance in the fighting arts, teaching tactics, and strategy. They tell about leadership, the value of inspiration and courage, and warn of the follies of recklessness or excessive caution. A student of military history can accumulate over 3,000 years of fighting experience at the price of time spent reading and analyzing the whispers of warriors past.

There are four practical lessons to be learned from the military professional by military history: fighting, generalship, innovation, and lessons learned. Beginning with lessons in fighting, each of these topics will be addressed in turn.

Lessons in Fighting

From the whispers of warriors, students of military history can gain an experiential foundation at all three levels of war—tactical, operational, and strategic. Junior officers should focus on tactics. After tactics have been mastered and as officers rise in seniority, they should also study the operational and strategic levels of war.

Tactical

Army Field Manual 7–8, *Infantry Rifle Platoons and Squads*, states: "Mission tactics require that leaders learn how to think rather than what to think. It recognizes that the subordinate is often the only person at the point of decision who can make an informed decision."[1]

Tactics are based on doctrine, reinforced through repetition during training, staff rides, and exercises, and ultimately proven in combat. Knowledge of doctrine and rehearsal of tactics are essential elements in learning tactics. However, they still fall short in teaching a leader how to think in the face of the friction and fog of war, against an enemy intent on killing him, who comes to the battlefield with an entirely different set of weaponry, tactics, techniques and procedures, cultural motivation, and objectives. While still only a substitute for combat experience, through history a leader can learn the intricacies of how successful officers prevailed tactically against an adversary or, conversely, why they failed. More important, a reader of history can learn the background behind tactics and understand their development, allowing him to execute them in the proper context or innovate in the face of dynamic change. In short, a reader of military history learns how to think about tactics rather than what to think.

General George S. Patton, one of America's great tacticians, was an avid reader of history. He studied tactics intensely, in concert with learning everything he could of potential adversaries. As early as 1909, while still a cadet at the United States Military Academy, Patton wrote in his personal notebook:

> In order for a man to become a great soldier . . . it is necessary for him to be so thoroughly conversant with all sorts of military possibilities that when ever an occasion arises he has at hand without effort on his part a parallel. To attain this end . . . it is necessary . . . to read military history in its earliest and hence crudest form and to follow it down in natural sequence permitting his mind to grow with his subject until he can grasp without effort the most abstruse question of the science of war because he is already permeated with all its elements.[2]

By the time World War II erupted, Patton was tactically primed and ready. As Sun Tzu instructed, "Know the enemy and know yourself; in a hundred battles you will never be in peril," Patton studied his adversaries and their tactics as a matter of course. He maintained his study of the enemy during the conduct of campaigns.

The 1944 breakout from Normandy illustrates this point. Bad weather threatened to postpone an armywide general offensive against the Saar-Moselle triangle. When the time for the "go, no-go" decision came, Patton stuck to his order to attack. However, he fretted over his decision. In his diary he wrote: "Woke up at 0300 and it was raining like hell. I actually got nervous and got up and read Rommel's book, *Infantry Attacks*. It was most helpful, as he described all the rains he had in September, 1914, and also the fact that, in spite of the heavy rains, the Germans got along."[3] After learning that the Germans had managed in equally dreadful weather during World War I, Patton was revitalized.

Tactical lessons abound in military history. A study of William Fetterman's massacre in 1866 near Lodge Trail Ridge in Wyoming yields the fundamentals of the ambush from its greatest practitioners, the American Indians. The 1763 battle of Bushy Run, pitting American rangers and British troops against the Indians, provides not only a daring example of how to neutralize an ambush but also of how a complete envelopment and certain rout can be turned into a victory via a bold counterattack. The Revolutionary War battle at Cowpens in 1781 teaches a tactical application of the layered defense, coupled with the importance of matching the tactic to the terrain and capabilities of the troops. The VII Corps's textbook flanking of the Iraqi defense in *Desert Storm*, reminiscent of Stonewall

Jackson's smashing success against Joseph Hooker's right flank at Chancellorsville in 1863, provides students of military tactics with proven examples of the flanking maneuver. Those who study and analyze such historical examples gain vicarious battlefield experience and also learn how to think about tactics.[4]

Operational

In addition to learning how to think about operations, the student of military history can learn warfare principles and enduring warfare themes through study at the operational and strategic levels of war. As Sir A.P. Wavell, British field marshal and viceroy of India, told his officers:

> The real way to get value out of the study of military history is to take particular situations, and as far as possible, to get inside the skin of a man who made a decision, realize the conditions in which the decision was made, and then see in what way you could have improved on it.

General Douglas MacArthur understood operational art and also the principle of maneuver. His September 15, 1950, landing at Inchon—deep behind North Korean lines, culminating in a hammer-and-anvil decimation of communist forces between Seoul and Pusan—stands as one of the most brilliant and daring operations in the annals of warfare.[5]

MacArthur had firsthand combat experience to draw from in crafting the Inchon-Seoul campaign. He had orchestrated 87 amphibious assaults in the Pacific campaign against the Japanese during World War II. MacArthur, however, also drew from history. As Army Chief of Staff in 1935, he advised that the military student "extends his analytic interest to the dust-buried accounts of wars long past as well as those still reeking with the scent of battle" to "bring to light those fundamental principles, and their combinations and applications which, in the past, have been productive of success."

MacArthur operationalized the words of Carl von Clausewitz, written 118 years earlier: "A swift and vigorous transition to attack—the flashing sword of vengeance—is the most brilliant point of the defensive."

Strategic

Strategy is the domain of top-level decisionmakers, where military operations join with policy, politics, and national objectives. It requires a comprehensive understanding of national objectives and all means of national power—military, diplomatic, and economic—as the precursor to linking ends with means. Military history provides lessons in applied strategy.

Strategies employed in the conduct of war can be evaluated in terms of actual outcomes.

America's most renowned naval thinker, Alfred Thayer Mahan, said about strategy:

> As in a building, which, however fair and beautiful the superstructure, is radically marred and imperfect if the foundation be insecure—so, if the strategy be wrong, the skill of the general on the battlefield, the valor of the soldier, the brilliancy of victory, however otherwise decisive, fail of their effect.

Mahan's words prophetically describe Germany's failure in World War II against Russia. Germany's generals performed brilliantly. Her soldiers fought bravely and with great skill. Through blitzkrieg tactics, the Germans won many decisive victories in battle. Yet all came to naught for an ill-conceived strategy.

The roots of Germany's strategic problems can be traced back to the interwar years, when, paradoxically, they began a great military renaissance. After World War I, General Hans von Seeckt, chief of the German army command from 1920 to 1926, began a reformation of the German army, intent on correcting many of its World War I deficiencies. He began with training. He pushed the Army to adopt maneuver tactics, setting the stage for blitzkrieg. He built an effective, independent-thinking noncommissioned officer corps. Most important, he transformed officer training into officer education. Officers learned the specifics of their branch, including tactics and weaponry. They also studied subjects common to all branches, as well as military history. Many scholars, however, have criticized the otherwise stellar German officer training and education program for its lack of attention to grand strategy, politics, and economics.[6] The Wehrmacht felt that strategy was beyond its purview—instead, it focused on operational art.

The decades of dedication to the study of tactics, operations, and military history nonetheless paid off when World War II erupted. Germany fielded an army with officers who were masters of tactics and operations. Not surprisingly, they prevailed at the tactical and operational levels of war. However, their strategic prowess was not equal to their expertise in operational art. They left strategic decisions up to their commander in chief, Adolf Hitler.

By the time the Germans invaded Russia in June of 1941, Hitler was totally enamored with the blitzkrieg. After decisive blitzkrieg victories over Poland and France, he was convinced that the Red Army would quickly fold its tent once Operation *Barbarossa* began. But Hitler failed to grasp the strategic differences between a war in Europe and a war in Russia. Russia was different—bitter cold in the winter, opening to the east in a widening expanse that had swallowed the likes of Napoleon. Russia would once again trade space for time, which, coupled with her numerical superiority and fierce fighting spirit in defense of her homeland, would ground the lightning attack. Even with blitzkrieg tactics and great valor from its soldiers, the Wehrmacht failed to win Russia. Hitler would have done better to listen to the warning whispers of Napoleon.

A student of strategic history learns why Pericles' defensive strategy failed against the Spartans. He better understands the failure of the Confederate strategy to demoralize the North and entice European intervention against General Winfield Scott's Anaconda strategy.[7] The military scholar learns the conditions that necessitated a "Germany First" strategy during World War II and to appreciate the economic and diplomatic sides of war, as evidenced by the success of the containment strategy used against the Soviet Union during the Cold War.

Lessons in Generalship

Generalship refers to the military skill of a high commander. In addition to knowledge of strategy, operations, and tactics, great generalship requires personal courage in the face of danger, the ability to inspire and move armies and fleets, and the ability to weigh risks and remain clearheaded in the face of chaos.[8] Military history provides a wealth of case studies in generalship.

Leadership

While the study of the campaigns of the great captains will yield lessons in fighting, the study of the great captains themselves can augment a military officer's knowledge of leadership. Their courage in the face of fire, their inspirational exhortations, their bold and audacious actions, forever stand as leadership examples, no matter the era or service affiliation.

The leadership styles of the great generals and admirals have been as different as their names and personalities. From soft-spoken to loud and booming, from conceptual thinkers to detailed planners, leaders have varied greatly in character and leadership styles. Although their styles have defied condensation into a universal set of personality traits, students of military history can hone their own styles from study of great captains with styles similar to their own. From experience forged in battle, their counsel on leadership is as important a part of their legacy as their results in battle.

Superior leadership and martial wisdom alone do not complete the skill required for generalship. In combination with leadership, pervasive knowledge of strategy and tactics, and the trust and confidence of subordinates, the great captains also knew how to take appropriate risks. The study of military history provides case studies in risk calculation in which the gravest of stakes were on the line. As the great humanist Erasmus said, "Fortune favors the audacious." This statement applies to all of the great captains. Contrarily, hardship curses the reckless and overly cautious.

The Audacious

Napoleon described Hannibal as "the most audacious of all, probably the most stunning, so hardy, so sure, so great in all things." Hannibal's crossing of the Alps to attack the Romans in Italy, for which he is principally known, stands as perhaps the most audacious act in all of military history. The trek was not without its costs. Hannibal lost almost half his original force of 46,000 men and all but a few of the 38 elephants he started with. Nonetheless, Hannibal's crossing of the Alps also had its payoffs. Hannibal achieved a string of military successes against superior odds, culminating in one of the most storied battles of all time—the battle of Cannae.

Two Roman double-consular armies met Hannibal on open ground near Cannae. The Romans outnumbered Hannibal's forces and looked to outflank Hannibal on both sides. Hannibal aligned his troops in a crescent formation, with the wings curved away from the Roman lines. The Romans attacked the Carthaginian infantry center, which gave way before them, allowing the Roman infantry to encircle them. The Roman infantry, sensing victory, closed in for the kill. On the wings, however, the Carthaginian cavalry had defeated the Roman cavalry and maneuvered to turn the crescent formation inside out to envelop the Roman infantry. Hannibal's army slaughtered the Roman armies. Hannibal had audaciously taken on a superior force and defeated it with a double-envelopment maneuver that is still studied today.

The Cautious

General "Fighting Joe" Hooker at Chancellorsville serves as an example of how excessive caution can turn an otherwise brilliant commander into a beaten man. In the spring of 1863, the Confederates held 25 miles of unbroken, fortified lines in Virginia, from Port Royal to Banks Ford. Robert E. Lee still held Marye's Heights in Fredericksburg, scene of Ambrose Burnside's earlier thrashing. Hooker realized that in spite of his two-to-one superiority over the Army of Northern Virginia, another attack on Fredericksburg would end with the same devastating results. Instead, Hooker planned to flank Lee's army by an upstream crossing of the Rappahannock and Rapidan Rivers with three corps, while holding Lee in place with 40,000 men at Fredericksburg. The plan proceeded smoothly until Union forces began to encounter resistance leaving the Wilderness toward Fredericksburg. Thanks to J.E.B. Stuart's cavalry probes, Lee had caught wind of Hooker's plan and sent 50,000 men to take on Hooker. Lee, an audacious general in his own right, dangerously split his force again, sending Stonewall Jackson's corps to flank Hooker's right side. With Lee's forces split, Hooker had an opportunity to counterattack and crush the Confederate forces. Instead, Hooker lost his nerve and cautiously ordered a withdrawal to Chancellorsville. With that order, Hooker handed over the reins of initiative to Lee, snatching defeat from the jaws of victory.

The Reckless

Everyone knows the story of Custer's last stand and his headlong reckless rush after the Indians. Another, lesser-known Indian battle, the battle of Blue Licks, also serves to highlight the difference between reckless and audacious action. In August 1782, a group of 182 Kentucky militiamen, led by Colonel John Todd and including members of the Boone family, was in hot pursuit of Indians who had attacked an American fort.[9] One officer, Major Hugh McGary, advised Colonel Todd to wait for reinforcements. Todd rebuked McGary for his timidity, a scorn that did not sit well with the hotheaded company commander.

During the pursuit, Daniel Boone noticed the Indians were concealing their numbers by sharing tracks, yet making the trail very easy to follow. Boone smelled an ambush by a force he estimated at 500 Indians. The rangers caught up to the Indians at the Blue Licks. Several Indian warriors showed themselves at the top of the rocky hilltop. Boone knew the terrain. At the top of the hilltop were wooded ravines that could shield an Indian force from view. He advised breaking off the pursuit. McGary, still stinging from Todd's previous insult, called Boone a coward. He leapt onto his horse, yelling, "Them that ain't cowards follow me," and recklessly charged into the river toward the Indians. Colonel Todd and the rest of the rangers followed. The Indians were indeed waiting in ambush, just as Boone feared. The rangers suffered a devastating defeat, in which Daniel Boone lost his son, Israel.[10] Rather than provide inspiration at the decisive moment, McGary had recklessly incited a charge outside of the proper context.

Inspiration

Military history smiles most brightly on its most brilliant generals who were also monuments to inspiration. American military history has many proud examples of inspirational leadership. John Paul Jones revitalized his badly beaten crew in the battle between the HMS *Serapis* and the *Bon Homme Richard* with his reply, "I have not yet begun to fight," to the British call for surrender. Major General Anthony C. McAuliffe's simple yet defiant reply of "Nuts!" to the German demand for surrender at Bastogne steeled not only the hearts of the defending 101st Airborne and 10th Armored Divisions but also the rest of the American army in northwest Europe.[11] Inspirational words coupled with courage, and the strong will of a great captain, can turn the tide of battle. They can move men to victory against superior odds, just as Lord Horatio Nelson's signal that "England expects that every man will do his duty" did for his fleet on October 21, 1805, at the battle of Trafalgar.

Study of the great captains yields the context and timing of tide-turning remarks and shows the power of inspiration through the force of their results. While few officers will ever find themselves in situations like those of Jones off Flamborough Head, McAuliffe in Bastogne, or Nelson at Trafalgar—with fewer still the headiness to articulate such elegant, fiery prose in the midst of carnage—strong-willed officers must still be able to buttress the fighting spirit of their troops and move them to action. Inspiration can mean the difference between victory and defeat.

Inspiration can also result from deed and attitude rather than words. In Lord Moran's *The Anatomy of Courage*, Surgeon Commander McDowell provides a compelling account of inspirational leadership, while also noting its personal toll on the leader:

> I saw the Captain of a ship drinking a cup of tea on the bridge in the course of dive-bombing attacks that had gone on all day. While he was drinking the lookout reported "Aircraft on the starboard bow, sir." He did not even look up. At "Aircraft diving, sir," the Captain glanced up only. "Bomb released, sir," and the Captain gave the order "Hard a-starboard," and went on drinking his tea until the bomb hit the water nearby. The reaction to this episode was a kind of hero-worship on the part of everyone who saw it. When the bombing had ceased the Captain went down to his cabin and when he was alone he wept.

Courage

Generalship requires courage—the strength to persevere in the face of fear. Of all the military virtues, it is the most prized and highly rewarded. No man knows how he will react to the stresses of combat until actually tested in battle. More likely than not, he will grapple with his own fear of death, while trying his best to present a mask of courage. History whispers the accounts of the great captains, who sometimes shared the fact that they too had to overcome personal fear in the face of combat. In a March 25, 1943, letter to his wife, Beatrice, Patton admitted, "I still get scared under fire. I guess I will never get used to it, but I still poke along." Untested warriors can take solace in the fact that fear is normal, a precondition to courageous action.

Commanders must also have the moral courage to do what is right in spite of popular sentiment or even orders. The whispers of the 109 civilians massacred at the Vietnamese village of My Lai at the orders of Lieutenant William Calley on March 16, 1968, still remind us of a higher duty always to do what is right.

Lessons in Innovation

We must stay tuned to the whispers of history—they must not be drowned out by crescendo of the present. As Sir Julian Corbett noted, "The value of history in the art of war is not only to elucidate the resemblance of past and present, but also their essential differences." The development of the German blitzkrieg between World War I and World War II illustrates Corbett's insight.

World War I defensive victories in battles such as Verdun, as opposed to the slaughter of French soldiers in offensive operations, led the French to believe that an impenetrable Maginot line would protect the French from future aggression. The lesson learned by the French was right, that in World War I the defense dominated. The Germans learned the same lesson. But whereas the French adopted the lesson, the Germans adapted to it.

At the close of World War I, the Germans had some success with their elite stormtroop units in overcoming the stalemate of static trench warfare. They studied stormtroop tactics, looking for ways to improve them. While the stormtroop units were able to take advantage of surprise and speed to overcome enemy defensive positions, they still were short of the mobility required to take advantage of their gains. During the years following World War I, the Germans developed the blitzkrieg concept, a mobile form of warfare that combined close air support with tanks and mechanized infantry, to shift the advantage back to the offensive.

Lessons in Lessons Learned

History teaches that every war is unique. "Lessons learned" typically focus on what worked—and what did not—in the last conflict. History is replete with examples of militaries staying with successful technology and doctrine from previous conflicts only to suffer disastrous results in the next.

History also teaches that there are no silver bullets in warfare. Multiple means are necessary to address a spectrum of conflict that continues to expand with each evolution and revolution in warfare. The debate over the utility of the atomic bomb after the bombings at Hiroshima and Nagasaki is a case in point. After the surrender of the Japanese in World War II, air extremists proclaimed that the atomic bomb rendered all other weapons and forces obsolete.[12] They argued that the dropping of the bomb at Hiroshima and Nagasaki heralded the nuclear age, in which traditional forms of power projection—to include the Army, Navy, and Marines—were relics of the past. The atomic bomb could do it all—the Nation merely needed to invest in bombers and A-bombs. An acrimonious debate culminated in 1949 with a special House Armed Services Committee investigation.[13]

The committee report debunked the myth of the "one-weapon, easy-war concept"; it was further underscored when the North Koreans attacked across the 38th parallel on June 25, 1950. Strategic bombing with atomic weapons was simply not an option. The Korean War was a bloody conflict in which ground forces, supported by air and sea power, were the final arbiters.

Conclusion

Serious study of history is essential to the development of exceptional military professionals. Napoleon, on his way to exile at Saint Helena, probably summed it up best in referring to his own son's education: "My son should read and meditate often about history; the only true philosophy. And he should read and think about the great captains. This is the only way to learn about war."

On a personal note, I still have my father's hat. I no longer wear it; even so, I know the whispers of the past still reside within it. I remember their lessons. My father's hat reminds me. . . .

Notes

[1] Field Manual 7–8, *Infantry Rifle Platoons and Squads* (Washington, DC: Department of the Army, 1992), chapter 2, "Operations."

[2] Martin Blumenson, *Patton: The Man Behind the Legend, 1885–1945* (New York: William Morrow, 1985).

[3] Martin Blumenson, *The Patton Papers, 1940–1945* (New York: Da Capo, 1996).

[4] To find out more about these battles, the following readings are recommended: Roy E. Appleman, "The Fetterman Fight," in *Great Western Indian Fights*, ed. Potomac Corral of the Westerners (Lincoln: University of Nebraska Press, 1960, repr. 1966), chap. 10; Mark M. Boatner, *Encyclopedia of the American Revolution* (New York: David McKay, 1966); Thomas Fleming, "The Cowpens," *Military History Quarterly* (Summer 1989), 56–67; Victor Davis Hanson, "Cannae," *Military History Quarterly* (Summer 1990), 60–65; Alberto Bin, Richard Hill, and Archer Jones, *Desert Storm: A Forgotten War* (Westport: Praeger, 1998); and Stephen W. Sears, *Chancellorsville* (Boston: Houghton Mifflin, 1996).

[5] For more on the Korean War, see T.R. Fehrenbach, *This Kind of War: A Study in Unpreparedness* (Washington, DC: Brassey's, 1998).

[6] James S. Corum, *The Roots of Blitzkrieg: Hans von Seeckt and German Military Reform* (Lawrence: University Press of Kansas, 1992), 75–96.

[7] Allan R. Millett and Peter Maslowski, *For the Common Defense: A Military History of the United States of America* (New York: Free Press, 1984), 161.

[8] Napoleon advised that "the first quality for a commander in chief is a cool head, which receives a correct impression of things. He should not allow himself to be confused by either good or bad news. The impressions which he receives successively or simultaneously in the course of a day should classify themselves in his mind in such a way as to occupy the place which they merit, for reason and judgment are the result of the comparison of various impressions taken into consideration. There are men who, by their physical and moral make-up, create for themselves a complete picture built upon a single detail. Whatever knowledge, intelligence, courage and other good qualities such men may have, nature has not marked them for command of armies or for direction of great operations of war."

[9] Isaac Newton Skelton III and Earl Franklin Skelton, *Ike, This Is You* (Washington, DC: n.p., 1995), 132–141.

[10] The author's great-great-great grandfather, Squire Boone, was wounded in the thigh during the battle.

[11] S.L.A. Marshall, *Bastogne* (Washington, DC: Infantry Journal Press, 1946).

[12] Bertram Vogal, "A Reply to the Extremists," U.S. Naval Institute *Proceedings* (May 1947), 545–547.

[13] J. D. Hittle, "Korea: Back to the Facts of Life," U.S. Naval Institute *Proceedings* (December 1950), 1289–1297.

Chapter 9

It Ain't New:
Joint Operations

Unless history can teach us how to look at the future, the history of war is but a bloody romance.

—J. F. C. Fuller

A s ranking member of the House Armed Services Committee, I rely on the lessons of history to help me understand and reach decisions about the future of the Armed Forces of today. Over the years, I have discovered that most dilemmas the military faces are actually not new issues. Frequently, I find similar situations from the past to use as guideposts to frame the issues of today.

Some national security professionals, both civilian and military, think that a brand-new era of warfare is at hand. They believe that modern battles will be joint operations fought by loose coalitions of countries with various national interests. They also believe that U.S. Army, Navy, Air Force, and Marine Corps forces will use controversial weapons produced by 21st-century technological breakthroughs. In fact, true students of military history realize that these concepts—joint operations, coalition warfare, and the integration of new technology—have their roots in battles of yesteryear. They look to the past for lessons on how to fight today.

Joint Operations

The nature of modern warfare demands that we fight as a joint team. This was important yesterday, it is essential today, and it will be even more important tomorrow.

—General John Shalikashvili

Author's Note: I wish to express my gratitude to Major Mary F. O'Brien, USAF, for her insight and research contributions in the preparation of this article, first published in *Aerospace Power Journal* (Fall 2000).

I have noticed an increase in the number of people who assume that joint operations began after enactment of the Goldwater-Nichols Department of Defense Reorganization Act of 1986. Nothing could be further from the truth, although our most recent well-known and successful joint operation—*Desert Storm*—owes a great deal of its success to that important legislation. The truth is that the U.S. Armed Forces have a long tradition of cooperation among the services in order to accomplish their missions.

One of America's First Joint Operations: The Siege of Veracruz

For example, the siege of Veracruz in 1847 during the Mexican War was the most successful of many joint operations during that war.[1] This operation, planned and executed by the Army and Navy, represented the first major amphibious operation in American history and the largest one conducted until World War II. Major General Winfield Scott, the senior Army commander, developed a plan that was clearly joint in every sense of the word. He placed great reliance on the Navy in order to execute his plan, including the unprecedented step of putting Army transports temporarily under the command of Navy Commodore David Conner.[2] General Scott also created a joint procurement process and developed command and control procedures to allow the Army and Navy to communicate with each other during the operation. Army troops on the transport ships needed small landing craft in order to get ashore, so Scott had "surfboats" specifically constructed for the amphibious assault. Although these vessels were contracted through the Army quartermaster, a naval officer—Lieutenant George M. Totten—designed them.[3] In order to synchronize the Army and Navy effort, General Scott and Commodore Conner worked out a new set of signals for supporting fires, loading surfboats, and assaulting the beach because the existing signals assumed an all-Army invasion.[4] Once the Army troops assembled onshore, the Navy brought guns and personnel off the ships to Army emplacements in order to coordinate artillery efforts from ship- and land-based artillery. The landing and successful siege at Veracruz opened the way for more victories during the Mexican War, which resulted in the acquisition of additional U.S. territories.

A Modern-Day Joint Operation: *Desert Storm*

Nearly 150 years after the siege at Veracruz, General Norman Schwarzkopf of the U.S. Army commanded one of the most successful joint military operations in history. He planned to maximize the military services' unique capabilities at each stage of the campaign to defeat Iraq. The offensive air campaign phase of *Desert Storm* integrated Air Force, Navy, Marine, and—to some extent—Army airpower to strike critical Iraqi targets. His determination to use the best of what each service had to offer continued into the ground-campaign phase. On [February 24] G–Day, U.S. ground forces, consisting of two Army corps and a Marine expeditionary force, together with coalition ground forces, assembled more than 200,000 soldiers to face the Iraqis. Numerous ground-attack aircraft continued to bomb hostile artillery sites, armored units, supply vehicles, and troops. Naval forces also contributed to the ground offensive. Surface ships supported amphibious operations, and the USS *Missouri* (BB–63) and USS *Wisconsin* (BB–64) bombarded Iraqi coastal positions and provided naval gunfire support to advancing troops.[5]

General Schwarzkopf was instrumental in keeping the joint effort on track. When conflicts arose among the services over their roles, Schwarzkopf adjudicated their differences. Early in the conflict, for example, he had to settle a disagreement between the Navy and Air Force concerning beyond-visual-range rules of engagement for attacking hostile aircraft.[6] Fearing incidents of fratricide, the Air Force wanted a friendly aircraft to make two types of independent verification of hostility before its fighter aircraft launched air-to-air missiles. Since Navy aircraft could conduct only one type of verification, they wanted an airborne warning and control system (AWACS) aircraft to perform the second verification. Otherwise, Navy fighters could not use the Phoenix air-to-air missile at optimal range. The Air Force resisted using AWACS, believing that it did not provide an accurate location of hostile fighters when they flew in proximity to friendly aircraft. When Vice Admiral Stan Arthur and Lieutenant General Chuck Horner, the Navy and Air Force component commanders, respectively, could not reach an agreement, they asked General Schwarzkopf to make the final determination. He supported a modified Air Force position that resulted in both Admiral Arthur and General Horner continuing their good working relationship and respecting each other's viewpoints.[7]

One can examine the success of joint operations during *Desert Storm* by considering the relationship among General Schwarzkopf, the supporting commanders in chief (CINC), and the service chiefs. U.S. Transportation Command provided the logistics to get the necessary troops and equipment in-theater; U.S. Space Command warned of Scud missile launches, and its Global Positioning System satellites facilitated operations; and the geographic CINCs provided air, sea, and ground forces from their theaters. The service chiefs fulfilled their roles as force providers to

General Schwarzkopf, giving him all the well-trained and equipped forces he needed. They also acted as a source of information on how best to employ these forces without trying to interfere in the command relationships established by the Goldwater-Nichols Act.

Coalition Warfare

There is only one thing worse than fighting with allies—and that is fighting without them.

—Winston S. Churchill

The Department of Defense (DOD) has increased the emphasis on training and fighting with our allies, especially since the end of the Persian Gulf War. It is important to recognize that, because they lack either the support of world opinion or the military capabilities to operate independently, few countries can fight alone. The need for countries to form alliances based on common national interests or security concerns has existed for millennia.

The Duke of Marlborough: Skilled at Coalition Warfare

John Churchill, the duke of Marlborough, acted as commander of British, Dutch, Prussian, Danish, and other Grand Alliance forces during the War of the Spanish Succession, fighting four battles successfully against the French army from 1701 to 1712. For nearly 10 years, his personal diplomacy effort, unusual at the time, was the driving force behind the daunting task of keeping the incredibly fractious coalition together. Churchill understood that face-to-face meetings with allied rulers and ministers in Berlin, Vienna, and the Hague could prove more effective in resolving difficulties and formulating plans than written communication.[8] Because of his efforts, the allies gave him their confidence and trust as well as control of their armies.

Churchill's attempts to win over the members of the Grand Alliance paid off for him years later while he prepared for his last campaign against the French in 1711. When his enemies in England's new Parliament wanted to replace him, other leaders of the Grand Alliance spoke on his behalf. The duke of Hanover and the king of Prussia threatened to withdraw their troops unless he remained in command, which led the rest of the Grand Alliance to state their strong belief that he should continue to be in charge. They saw him as their champion, especially since he had already led the alliance to victory in three battles against the French.[9]

Wesley Clark: Leading NATO in Its First Fight as an Alliance

Maintaining a cohesive alliance or coalition today is just as important, if not more so, than in the past. As the Supreme Allied Commander, Europe, Army General Wesley Clark led the North Atlantic Treaty Organization (NATO) in its first military campaign, Operation *Allied Force* in mid-1999. In addition to trying to convince Yugoslav leader Slobodan Milosevic to pull his forces out of Kosovo, General Clark had to ensure that internal differences among NATO countries concerning the conduct of the campaign and the desired outcome did not pull NATO apart.

To General Clark, maintaining alliance cohesion during *Allied Force* was just as important as avoiding casualties, targeting Serb forces and associated targets, and minimizing collateral damage.[10] He had a difficult time keeping his targeting strategy on track because every target required unanimous approval of the allies, some of whom opposed the entire campaign or certain aspects of it. For example, Greece and Italy opposed an extended bombing campaign, France resisted plans for a naval blockade, and Germany opposed any consideration of a ground war.[11] General Clark had to rely on his diplomatic skills to convince NATO allies of the need to escalate the campaign and to consider the possibility of a ground war. He used personal phone calls and meetings to persuade them to reduce bombing constraints in order to intensify the campaign, yet maintain allied consensus and cohesion.[12]

In an effort to obtain approval of two particularly important targets—the Yugoslav Interior Ministry and the headquarters of the Serbian special police—General Clark personally briefed Javier Solana, NATO secretary general, on the intricacies of targeting. He included such details as the blast radius of warheads and how the desired point of impact controlled whether the building would collapse inward or explode outward. Clark thought it important to send a message by striking these targets during the first missions to Belgrade. The North Atlantic Council debated the request but in the end left the final decision to Secretary General Solana, who gave his approval a few days later.[13]

General Clark earned the admiration of NATO for his leadership in the Balkans. During the change-of-command ceremony for General Clark, Lord Robertson, Solana's successor as NATO secretary general, praised him for his "unique combination of military expertise, political knowledge, and diplomatic skill."[14] Lord Robertson went on to say that General Clark was "the right man in the right place at the right time" to lead the first major military offensive in the 50-year history of the alliance. General Clark's command ensured NATO success.

Allies with Unequal Military Capabilities Benefit from Unity

In addition to ensuring shared goals among the alliance nations, coalition warfare involves another concern. In the year since the end of the bombing over Serbia, the United States and the rest of the NATO countries have had an opportunity to study the lessons learned from the first NATO military operation. Among these many lessons, everyone emphasizes and agrees that the European countries have fallen behind the United States both militarily and technologically—a matter of great concern that NATO will address over the next few years. Again, this situation is not new to us, and we should not let it interfere with our reliance on our allies during times of crisis. There was a time in American history when the opposite was true—we Americans fielded the inexperienced, poorly equipped force and had to rely on the superior capabilities of our European allies.

Specifically, the American Continental Army largely owed its victory over superior British forces during the American Revolution to the military assistance of France, which sent officers, soldiers, gunpowder, and ships to the Americans. The commander of French forces in America also had a strong hand in shaping the objectives of the war. Jean-Baptiste-Donatien de Vimeur, comte de Rochambeau, argued for an attack on Lord Charles Cornwallis in the south despite General George Washington's desire to lay siege to New York instead.[15] The comte de Rochambeau had already begun planning for a siege at Yorktown when he requested assistance from the commander of the French fleet in the Caribbean. Admiral François-Joseph-Paul de Grasse responded by canceling all other missions, readying every ship, obtaining troops and field artillery, borrowing money, and immediately setting sail for the American coast. The tremendous support for the operation at Yorktown convinced General Washington to march his troops south instead of north to New York.

Meanwhile, the French defeated the British fleet off the Virginia coast, ensuring that Lord Cornwallis would not receive the reinforcements he urgently needed from New York. The allied army began preparations for the offensive, supported by the accurate bombardment of the British by the French cannoneers. American and French troops successfully attacked, forcing Lord Cornwallis to surrender. British reinforcements arrived 5 days later, but the French fleet still controlled the Chesapeake. The British returned to New York without engaging French forces.[16] Despite the disparity in expertise, the American and French military efforts complemented one another. The Americans fought for freedom and the birth of a nation, while the French brought the necessary professionalism, technical expertise, and equipment.

Operation *Allied Force*: American Military Technology Pulls Ahead

It quickly became clear during *Allied Force* that U.S. military capabilities have dramatically pulled ahead of those of our European allies. The Kosovo after-action report to Congress noted this gap, especially in the areas of precision strike; mobility; and command, control, and communications.[17] This forced the United States to conduct the majority of the precision strike sorties, especially during the first days of the conflict when the Yugoslav air defenses remained fully operational. As it became clear to the NATO political and military leadership that the United States would bear the brunt of the cost of the military effort, the allies agreed that the Europeans would cover the majority of the cost of the peace enforcement and reconstruction efforts in Kosovo. Although the exact division of costs is the subject of spirited debate, the Europeans seem to be living up to their promise.

Even though the United States led the military effort during *Allied Force*, we could not have carried out the entire operation without assistance from our European allies, who provided personnel, equipment, and—more important—political and diplomatic support. One should also note that the United States benefited from use of the NATO allies' military infrastructure, including military bases, airfields, and airspace. Although the B–2 bomber proved very effective in operating from Whiteman Air Force Base in Missouri, aircraft usually must launch from a location much closer to the theater in order to accomplish their mission. For that reason, U.S. forces deployed to facilities in countries closer to Kosovo and Serbia—such as Italy, the United Kingdom, Germany, Spain, France, Hungary, and others.

However, the gap in military capability—certainly a reason for concern and a topic of discussion at the summit recognizing the 50th anniversary of NATO—could affect future alliance efforts. To reduce this gap, NATO adopted the Defense Capabilities Initiative, which seeks to enhance allied capabilities in deployability and mobility; sustainability and logistics; effective engagement; survivability of forces and infrastructure; and command, control, and information systems. The overall goal is to improve interoperability between U.S. military forces and the rest of NATO.

Integrating Technological Innovations into the Military

We must be the great arsenal of democracy.

—Franklin D. Roosevelt

DOD feels strongly, as do some Members of Congress, that other nations can overcome the technological advantage long enjoyed by the United States if we do not continue to invest in research and development and field the weapon systems resulting from these efforts. Counterarguments come from those who believe that, although we eventually will have to modernize, our technological lead is so great now and for the foreseeable future that we can afford to take a breather from a policy of constant modernization. Congress is charged with finding the balance between the two sides. Unfortunately, this is not a simple exercise, and we will measure the consequences of being wrong in the loss of America's sons and daughters. I find it helpful to look to history to study another time when the United States faced a similar situation.

The current debate concerning precision warfare and the role it should play in future conflicts has a strong precedent in the integration of the airplane into the U.S. military. Prior even to the debates about establishing the Air Force as a separate branch of the armed services, controversy existed over the capabilities and limitations of the airplane and the role it should play. The airplane and precision-guided weapons are parallel issues almost 100 years apart, with consequences affecting doctrine, operations, tactics, and certainly, resource priorities.

Airplanes: Discovering Their Military Usefulness

The introduction of the aircraft to the U.S. military did not proceed smoothly. Many political and military leaders failed to see the need to expend resources to develop military aviation to its fullest potential. After World War I, Army leaders for the most part considered the airplane little more than another form of reconnaissance and artillery, and the United States did not follow Great Britain's example in establishing a separate air force. As the United States began to focus on domestic spending after the war, Generals Henry "Hap" Arnold and William "Billy" Mitchell began a public-relations campaign around the country to increase support for funding the Air Service. The support generated by their demonstrations forced the Navy to agree to a bombing test in 1921. After modifying the official rules of the test, Air Service pilots sank three captured German vessels, including the "unsinkable" battleship *Ostfriesland*. Two years later, the Air Service successfully repeated the tests by sinking two obsolete American battleships. Despite these achievements, the tests failed to gain any significant funding from Congress.

In addition to demonstrating the potential military capabilities of the airplane, early airpower advocates began to develop airpower theory, doctrine, and tactics. The Air Corps Tactical School at Maxwell Air Force Base, Alabama, is generally credited with considering the early airpower theories espoused by Mitchell, General Jugh Trenchard, and perhaps General Giullio Douhet—and with establishing the first airpower doctrine developed in the United States.[18] This doctrine advocated precision, high-altitude, daylight strategic bombardment against the enemy military-industrial complex. However, its publication did not convince skeptics in Congress—or the Army and Navy—of the usefulness of airpower. Only the success of actual strategic-bombardment missions and support to the ground troops during World War II convinced naysayers of the value of military missions for the airplane—and of the need for an independent Air Force.

Surprisingly, remnants of the debate about the role of airpower and its ability to play a decisive role in conflict continue in Congress and the Pentagon today, despite the critically important airpower demonstrations in both *Desert Storm* and *Allied Force*. The airplane now performs an extensive array of missions for all of the services, and I would not want to fight an adversary without the best aircraft America can produce.

Precision-Guided Weapons: Living Up to Their Promise

Today, I see many similarities between the struggle for acceptance of the airplane and the way the Armed Forces are integrating precision-guided munitions (PGMs) into the force structure. The effort to achieve more accurate weapons began in World War I and approached modern capabilities with PGMs toward the end of the Vietnam War. However, not until *Desert Storm* did the American public get a close-up view of the capability of PGMs. Increased emphasis on precision will drive changes in military doctrine, operations, and tactics. Already, it is clear that we need to make our intelligence, surveillance, and reconnaissance capabilities more responsive and accurate in order to support the efficient targeting of precision-guided weapons. Other questions remain concerning their roles, compared to that of traditional weapon systems, and the impact they will have on other military concepts, such as maneuver.

Each of the services must examine the part of their warfighting doctrine that addresses precision-guided weapons and develop the best plan for employing precision capability. They need to answer questions about when to use these weapons and against what types of targets. They should be able to answer critics logically who claim that striking a $50,000 target with a $1 million missile is unjustified, whether it is based on reducing risk to our servicemembers, the unique importance of the target, or some other factor. That done, the Pentagon must educate American leaders and the general public about these new weapons. Just as education about the airplane many years ago led to building the world's greatest air force, so does the Nation need to learn the capabilities and limitations of precision-guided weapons in order to understand why they represent a wise investment for the future.[19]

We need educational efforts not only to justify resources but also to employ PGMs against critical targets effectively. For example, during *Desert Storm*, coalition political and military leaders hesitated to allow the bombing of high-value targets located in or near population centers. However, after receiving briefings detailing the accuracy of PGMs, these leaders felt more comfortable using them against targets in cities.[20] As previously mentioned, General Clark gave the same types of briefings during *Allied Force* in order to gain NATO consensus to bomb certain targets in highly populated areas.

Conclusion

My study of history tells me that the challenges facing the military today—and into the future—are not new. The U.S. military must continue to develop leaders who understand *jointness* in order to fight as a joint force. This is important because the Nation needs the strength created when all of the armed services work together. In addition, because America will continue to lead and participate in coalitions, the services must prepare military leaders of tomorrow to operate comfortably in a *multinational environment*. They must understand the different national interests that may drive their counterparts and must recognize allied military capabilities in order to get the most out of their contributions. Finally, the United States cannot afford to integrate haphazardly *new technology* into its force structure. We must look ahead in order to understand the potential implications of technology and to ensure that theory, doctrine, and strategy do not fall behind. One of the best ways for future military leaders to prepare is to study military history. It might surprise them to discover how much yesteryear has in common with today. In other words—it ain't new.

Notes

[1] Paul C. Clark, Jr., and Edward H. Moseley, "Veracruz, 1847—A Grand Design," *Joint Force Quarterly* 10 (Winter 1995–1996), 104.

[2] K. Jack Bauer, *Surfboats and Horse Marines: U.S Naval Operations in the Mexican War, 1846–48* (Annapolis: U.S. Naval Institute, 1969), 77–78.

[3] Clark and Moseley, 108.

[4] Ibid., 100.

[5] U.S. Department of Defense, *Conduct of the Persian Gulf Conflict: Final Report to the Congress* (Washington, DC: Government Printing Office, April 1992), 293.

[6] P. Mason Carpenter, "Joint Operations in the Gulf War: An Allison Analysis" (thesis, School of Advanced Airpower Studies, Maxwell Air Force Base, AL, June 1994), 18–19.

[7] Ibid.

[8] J.R. Jones, *Marlborough* (Cambridge: Cambridge University Press, 1993), 138.

[9] Winston S. Churchill, *Marlborough: His Life and Times* (New York: Charles Scribner's Sons, 1968), 795.

[10] Wesley K. Clark, "The United States and NATO: The Way Ahead," *Parameters* 29, no. 4 (Winter 1999–2000), 7.

[11] Daniel L. Byman and Matthew C. Waxman, "Kosovo Reconsidered: NATO's Bombs and Belgrade's Strategy—Kosovo and the Great Air Power Debate," *International Security* 24, no. 4 (Spring 2000), 34.

[12] Dana Priest, "The Battle inside Headquarters," *The Washington Post*, September 21, 1999.

[13] Ibid.

[14] Linda D. Kozaryn, "Europe Salutes Allied Force Commander," American Forces Press Service, May 4, 2000; accessed at <http://www.defenselink.mil/news/May2000/n05042000_20005043.html>.

[15] Stephen C. Danckert, "The Siege of Yorktown: Coalition Force," *Military Review* 73, no. 1 (January 1993), 16.

[16] Ibid., 20.

[17] U.S. Department of Defense, *Kosovo/Operation* Allied Force *After-Action Report: Report to Congress* (Washington, DC: Government Printing Office, January 31, 2000), 25.

[18] James A. Mowbray, "Air Force Doctrine Problems: 1926–Present," *Airpower Journal* 9, no. 4 (Winter 1995), 3.

[19] Richard P. Hallion, "Precision Weapons, Power Projection, and the Revolution in Military Affairs," USAF Air Armament Summit, Eglin Air Force Base, FL, May 26, 1999; accessed at <http://www.airforcehistory.hq.af.mil/Hallionpapers/precisionweaponspower.htm>.

[20] Ibid.

Chapter 10

Military Lessons from
Desert One to the Balkans

The performance of the Armed Forces has shown a marked improvement since its low point in the post-Vietnam era. Military leaders have deliberately sought out and internalized lessons from each succeeding conflict. The challenge for the next generation is learning the lessons of these past operations and building an even more effective, flexible force. These lessons include the following:

■ The military cannot pick and choose its missions. Their political masters may well decide that national interests require the use of force for more nontraditional missions or in situations that may be less than ideally suited to military solutions.

■ Force protection is critical; high rates of casualties can erode popular support and undermine the mission. On the other hand, excessive fear of casualties can erode the morale of the Armed Forces. The key is forging American leadership that understands the military risks involved.

■ Commitments to our allies may draw us into conflicts where U.S. national interests are limited, but where American leadership is essential to the vitality of the alliance.

■ Even a small operation conducted abroad requires an extraordinary range of well-trained forces, either highly deployable or already in theater.

■ Despite successes, the Armed Forces must address a number of challenges: urban warfare, weapons of mass destruction, tracking and destroying mobile targets, the need for lighter, more deployable forces, and the burden of ongoing operations.

The original version of this chapter was published as *Strategic Forum* 174 (Washington, DC: Institute for National Strategic Studies, October 2000).

Military leaders are often accused, usually unfairly, of fighting the last war. It would be a pretty poor general, however, who failed to learn from what did and did not work when military plans were actually put to the test. The task is to correct what went wrong and to build on what went right without losing sight of the fact that conflicts in the future may be quite different from those in the past. It is the premise of this chapter that a careful look at significant U.S. military operations over about the past 20 years—roughly the period the author has served in Congress—can help shape answers to a surprisingly large number of contemporary issues in defense policy. What follows is a brief review of seven of these military operations, followed by a discussion of some important lessons.

Iran (1980)

President Jimmy Carter authorized an audacious military operation in April 1980 to rescue American diplomats held hostage in Tehran since the previous November. Although the operation ended in disaster in the Iranian desert at a site code-named *Desert One*, it ultimately had important consequences. It prompted a great deal of public soul-searching about the state of U.S. military readiness, and, perhaps most importantly, it marked a turning point in popular support for military preparedness. The lessons of *Desert One* also contributed to steps that Congress took in coming years to strengthen special operations forces and clarify lines of command.

Lebanon (1982–1984)

U.S. Marines were sent to Lebanon in September 1982 as part of a multinational force (MNF) in response to a worsening civil war. The failure of the MNF mission, and the tragic loss of 241 marines when a truck bomb was exploded at Marine headquarters in Beirut, imposed sobering lessons on U.S. policymakers. The mission was ill-defined from the beginning. It was not clear whether the MNF was a traditional peacekeeping force depending for its effectiveness on maintaining the consent of contending parties, or whether it was a peacemaking force empowered to compel adherence to agreements more assertively. The rules of engagement governing the conduct of troops in the field were ambiguous, and actions necessary to protect the force were not taken. As the security situation deteriorated, it should have become apparent that the size and composition of the force were inadequate, but decisionmakers failed to rethink the nature of the mission and instead allowed U.S. involvement to escalate incrementally.

The outcome of that mission shaped subsequent U.S. debates about the use of military force. Lebanon was clearly at the forefront of Secretary of Defense Caspar Weinberger's thinking when, in November 1984, he articulated what came to be known as the Weinberger doctrine, laying out six restrictive conditions on U.S. military action. Weinberger's sharpest critic was Secretary of State George Shultz, who in a series of three speeches took issue with most of those conditions. Echoes of their exchange are heard frequently in debates over military operations.

Grenada (1983)

Operation *Urgent Fury* in Grenada was planned with virtually no advance warning and executed by diverse units with no opportunity to train jointly before the operation began. Though it succeeded, it was not a walkover. The operation suffered from shortcomings that cost lives. Intelligence was incomplete, and communications were often unreliable, particularly in coordinating air attacks and naval gunfire with ground operations.

Perhaps the most important lesson of Grenada is the value of bold, concerted, aggressive military action, even in the face of incomplete intelligence and in spite of the certainty that some things will go wrong. In this operation, aggressiveness contributed to a viable overall strategic plan, which enabled American forces to perform very well in a very demanding operation.

Panama (1989–1990)

Despite some negatives, the main lessons of this operation against the Panamanian Defense Force and General Manuel Noriega were overwhelmingly positive. The cohesiveness of Operation *Just Cause* demonstrated the effectiveness of joint planning and command structures instituted following enactment of the Goldwater-Nichols Defense Reorganization Act of 1986. Simultaneous, coordinated assaults, using forces from each of the services, multiplied the impact of the whole operation. The action achieved a large measure of tactical surprise. The fact that the initial, critical stages of the intervention were carried out at night was particularly significant. As one commander noted, "We owned the night." Unmatched night-fighting capabilities have constituted a major U.S. tactical advantage ever since. Panama was clearly a case in which adequate force was applied to accomplish well-defined objectives with minimal casualties.

Persian Gulf (1990–1991)

The Persian Gulf War demonstrated the remarkable reconstitution of U.S. military power in the 15 years following an institutionally devastating failure in Vietnam. In all, 541,000 U.S. military personnel were committed to Operation *Desert Storm*, along with some 200,000 allied forces. Not surprisingly, given the size, complexity, and importance of the conflict, the effort to draw appropriate lessons has been extensive, and it continues to this day.

The most obvious conclusion is that no nation today can directly challenge U.S. conventional military strength, and it would be folly to try—a lesson our potential foes are certain also to have learned. Beyond that, the conflict demonstrated the efficacy of precision munitions; the success of stealth technology; the critical importance of air supremacy; the advantages of night operations; the ability of air power, under the right conditions, to disable an enemy command and control infrastructure; the immense importance of sound military doctrine and operational tenets derived from a careful study of past conflicts; the critical importance of unified command; the advantages of a well-trained professional military force; the value of attack helicopters, close support aircraft, and a number of other platforms when used creatively and with a full understanding of their potential vulnerabilities; the critical importance of information dominance; and the absolute necessity of good diplomacy in managing relations with allies and in deflecting serious outside challenges to the cohesiveness of a broad coalition. On all these diverse matters, the critical lesson is to keep doing what we have been doing.

There are some other, more cautionary lessons to be learned, however. The vulnerability of U.S. forces—and of critical allies—to weapons of mass destruction was a matter of grave concern. In the end, deterrence seems to have worked, but we need to consider whether it might fail in different circumstances. An immense effort was devoted to hunting down mobile missile launchers, but with no success at all. *Desert Storm* showed that much work remained to be done to provide critical intelligence immediately and directly to the forces that need it. While command and control arrangements worked very well by previous standards, air tasking orders had to be put on paper and flown out to aircraft carriers every day—not the way, in the information age, to carry out a complex, multidimensional campaign.

Finally, and perhaps most importantly, before Operation *Desert Storm* began, the United States and its allies had almost 5 months to build up military forces in the region. No enemy in the future is likely to allow us such a luxury.

Bosnia (1992–)

In June 1992, elements of the United Nations Protection Force were deployed to Bosnia to help restrain a growing civil war. As the civil war worsened and the situation deteriorated further, the United States had a very difficult time deciding how much involvement its interests warranted. Lack of American leadership risked weakening the North Atlantic Treaty Organization (NATO). Until the last half of 1995, half-hearted NATO efforts at coercive diplomacy, including the use of "pin-prick" air strikes, accomplished almost nothing.

A more extensive application of air power in Operation *Deliberate Force*, in contrast, was highly successful. Coupled with a Bosnian government ground offensive, it succeeded in forcing the Bosnian Serbs to make critical territorial concessions at the negotiating table. With U.S. leadership, NATO finally managed to forge a peace agreement and salvage its shaken credibility. The ongoing peace operation in Bosnia has also been largely successful. Assurances that U.S. troops would be withdrawn within a year were not realistic, however, and the operation now appears open-ended. Cuts in the size of the peacekeeping force and extensive use of reserves in Bosnia have had some effect in ameliorating the burden. But Bosnia—and now Kosovo—remain costly commitments.

Kosovo (1998–)

With Yugoslav government violence against ethnic Albanians in Kosovo mounting, on March 24, 1998, NATO began air strikes against targets in Serbia and Kosovo. President Clinton said that the objectives of Operation *Allied Force* were to demonstrate NATO seriousness of purpose, to deter an even bloodier offensive by Yugoslavia against innocent civilians in Kosovo, and, if necessary, to damage seriously the Serbian military capacity to make war in Kosovo. Instead of capitulating, however, Yugoslav forces intensified their operations in a massive ethnic cleansing campaign to drive ethnic Albanians out of Kosovo.

In response, NATO progressively escalated the pace of its air attacks and extended its target set. Target selection initially focused on airfields, air defense, and military communications. Attacks subsequently were expanded to military barracks and military equipment production facilities in Serbia, logistical support facilities and lines of supply throughout

Yugoslavia, Yugoslav forces in Kosovo, electrical transmission facilities, and television and other media outlets. Toward the end of the campaign, there appears to have been an effort to attack economic targets of particular value to Serbian leaders. Finally, on June 4, the Yugoslav government announced that it would accept a peace plan that called for an immediate cease-fire, withdrawal of all Yugoslav military and other security forces from Kosovo, deployment of an international peacekeeping force, and steps toward self-governance for Kosovo. On June 10, with evidence that Yugoslav forces were withdrawing, bombing ceased.

From the beginning of the campaign, the military logic of Operation *Allied Force* was a matter of intense, even bitter debate. In short, at least in its inception, the Kosovo air campaign was an exercise in coercive diplomacy rather than a concerted effort to prevail through military action by destroying the enemy capacity to wage war. And to the extent it became a warfighting exercise, it was much more a war of attrition than a modern U.S.-style application of decisive force. In this case, though, all of the attrition was on the other side. From the NATO point of view, this seems to have been enough, since Milosevic ultimately relented. It was not, however, enough to protect the Kosovars from the depredations of Yugoslav security forces.

The Current Debate

The value of reading and rereading history is not that old truths bear repeating, but that historical understanding is always new. Real events are always multifaceted and complex, and our perspectives on them always change when we view them through the prism of more recent experience. Looking back on these operations today turns out to be quite informative in discussing a number of contemporary issues. While others may distill different lessons from this brief review of recent military operations, here are a few perspectives that seem particularly relevant to current concerns.

Use of Force

Debate over whether and under what conditions to undertake military action is nothing new. Ongoing debates over the use of force have stirred in every administration and will likely have to be addressed anew by every future government. Those who take absolute positions—especially in disputes along partisan lines—are likely to have to swallow their arguments later. In debates about Bosnia and Kosovo, for example, some have taken the Weinberger doctrine almost as gospel. According to that doctrine, U.S. forces should be committed only when vital U.S. interests are at stake, when the mission is clear, when force fully and demonstrably adequate to accomplish the mission can be applied, and when public support is assured.

But that argument was vigorously disputed within the Reagan administration, particularly by then-Secretary of State George Shultz, from the moment it was articulated. Moreover, the Weinberger doctrine clearly did not prevail in later decisions on the use of force, even when Weinberger still led the Department of Defense.

For military commanders, the lesson is that they cannot pick and choose what missions to prepare for. Political leaders may well decide that national security interests require the use of force even in circumstances that give military planners fits, or that detract from other priorities, or that may cost lots of money at a time when funding is tight, or that risk unpredictable, bad consequences. This is not to say that commanders should simply salute and say "can do" when given any job. Political decisionmakers, too, should have learned that missions should be defined as clearly as possible. Adequate force should be applied. Force protection must be a high priority. Military commanders should properly point up all these lessons, but they cannot expect political leaders to agree, as one commentator would have it, that "superpowers don't do windows."

Fear of Casualties

There has been a vigorous discussion recently about the effects a fear of casualties may have on the ethos of U.S. military forces. Looking back a few years—beyond Kosovo and Bosnia—confirms that this is a very serious issue. Aggressiveness of American military commanders has often been critical to the success of the operations. Anything that might erode the elan of U.S. fighting forces, therefore, ought to be troubling. It is also true, however, that force protection is critically important. It was lacking in Lebanon, with disastrous effects. And aggressiveness cannot be disconnected from a viable strategy for prevailing.

It is tempting to draw an obvious conclusion: if a mission is not sufficiently important to U.S. national interests to warrant risking casualties, then it may not be worth doing at all, because casualties may erode popular support and cause the operation to fail anyway. But this is a bit too simple. Political leaders cannot avoid deciding on military action when public support is uncertain. Choosing a course of action that minimizes the risk of casualties even at a cost to military effectiveness may not always be unrealistic or unreasonable. The critical task is to accept risks when necessary and to avoid them when unnecessary, and to imbue U.S. military leaders, from the top of the chain of command to the bottom, with the wisdom to know the difference.

Relations with Allies

Relations with allies are never easy. Allies often perceive interests differently. And even when their interests and ours appear to coincide closely, history, domestic politics, varying military capabilities, and personal relationships among national leaders will affect the prospects for cooperation. One lesson of recent military operations is clear—the United States must be militarily and diplomatically flexible enough to cooperate with allies as much as possible, but also to act with limited allied support when necessary. As Winston Churchill put it so well: "There is only one thing worse than fighting with allies—and that is fighting without them."

Operations in Bosnia and Kosovo raise complex and controversial issues. One view is that the United States should not have become involved in either place because U.S. interests were not sufficiently at stake to justify the costs and risks of military action. But as Bosnia shows, when major allies have decided to act and the United States agrees with the goals of their action, it is very difficult for the United States to wash its hands of responsibility. Clearly the Bush administration did not want to get involved in leading a military campaign in Bosnia, and the Clinton administration tried to avoid it for another 2 ½ years. Having offered support to the allies in the first place, however, it became too difficult, perhaps even impossible, to allow the cause to fail. Ultimately, American leadership proved necessary. The lesson is that commitments to allies can draw the United States into conflicts where direct U.S. interests are limited, but where our interest in the continued vitality of the alliance may require American leadership. But it is hardly a startling notion that alliances have costs as well as benefits.

Across-the-Board Strength

Even apparently limited military operations have required a very broad range of well-trained and well-equipped forces. The interception of the *Achille Lauro* hijackers, a minor exercise of force not discussed in this chapter, was conceivable only because the United States had in place an extraordinarily varied number of critical elements: a highly effective global intelligence capability, including human intelligence and high-technology means of collection; air combat forces that could be deployed rapidly and flexibly; other air assets, including electronic warfare aircraft, already in place in the region to monitor sudden and unexpected developments; sophisticated radar, able to pick out aircraft rapidly in high air traffic already in place in the region; special operations forces that could be deployed on immediate notice and transport aircraft able to carry them 6,000 miles across the Atlantic; a global communications network that allowed planners in Washington immediate access to intelligence and unbroken links to forces in the region; a history of engagement with many nations in the area that allowed timely contact with key decisionmakers; and well-trained, well-motivated personnel in every one of these critical operational areas. All of this is expensive—the Nation cannot expect to have global reach on the cheap.

Things to Work On

While the United States has achieved a remarkable string of military successes in recent years, a review of past operations also shows some vulnerabilities. To their credit, the military services have recognized and have worked to correct a great many of them. Urban warfare is an obvious problem. Weapons of mass destruction may pose a disabling challenge to U.S. power projection capabilities, as the conflict with Iraq shows. We need a much deeper discussion of ways to ensure deterrence. Tracking down and destroying mobile targets remains an unresolved, serious problem. Though it may have been politically impossible to mount a ground operation in Kosovo that could have forestalled ethnic cleansing, it is critically important, nonetheless, to consider how a preemptive operation might have been mounted. The Army deserves credit for its current focus on building more deployable forces. Still, much remains to be resolved in determining precisely how lighter ground forces can accomplish critical missions.

An important unresolved issue is how to ameliorate the burden of ongoing operations, such as those in the Persian Gulf, in Bosnia, and now in Kosovo. Measures adopted to ease the burden have not gone far enough. Clearly there needs to be a discussion of more radical changes, including at least the strengthening of nonmilitary multinational institutions to take on the chore of nation-building and even the establishment of an international constabulary force for ongoing peacekeeping missions. Such steps have not been popular in Congress, but these or other measures need to be reconsidered.

We've Done a Lot Right

Perhaps the most important lesson is simply that the U.S. military has done a lot right. One can see in the conflicts reviewed here a progressive, substantial, lasting improvement in key capabilities, reflecting the willingness of the U.S. military to seek out and absorb the lessons of each new operation. The few years between Grenada and Panama, for example, witnessed improvements in command arrangements, operational planning, tactics and doctrine, training, and key technologies such as night vision equipment. The years between the Persian Gulf War and the Bosnia and Kosovo air campaigns showed the maturation of precision-strike capabilities. The Army and Air Force have both learned the need to be more readily deployable in an unpredictable global environment, and both are reorganizing substantially to become more flexible.

Congress, too, has sometimes helped. It established an independent Special Operations Command in 1987, an action that has been vindicated by the continued critical importance of special operations forces in a host of military actions since then, and by the marvelous performance of those forces when called upon. Congressional passage of the Goldwater-Nichols Department of Defense Reorganization Act of 1986 clearly helped to clarify and strengthen command arrangements.

The main praise for building an increasingly flexible and effective force, however, must go to the military officers who rebuilt U.S. military capabilities after the Vietnam War. This generation has now almost entirely reached retirement age. The task of the next generation of military leaders is to learn as well as its predecessors learned from past conflicts.

Chapter 11

America's Frontier Wars: Lessons for Asymmetric Conflict

In July 1755, Major General Edward Braddock, commander in chief of all British forces in North America and a 45-year career soldier, was killed along with 900 of his men by a smaller French and Indian force. On his way to capture Fort Duquesne, Pennsylvania, Braddock had split his force into two divisions. Because of the difficulty of crossing the wilderness, they opened a distance of 60 miles between the "flying column" division of rapidly moving soldiers and a support column hauling "monstrously heavy eight-inch howitzers and twelve-pound cannons" completely unsuited to the terrain.

The lead column stretched a mile in length and was attacked on the far side of the Monongahela River by Indians streaming along either British flank and hiding within the forest they had long used as hunting grounds. The British responded using traditional tactics—continuously trying to form companies and return fire but only concentrating their number further for Indian attack. Braddock ordered forward the main body of his troops, which then collided with retreating elements ahead. In the resulting confusion, 15 of the 18 officers in the advance party were picked off. Still, the remaining forces continued to fight the way they were taught: maintaining platoon formations and firing together even as they drew heavy fire to the line from well-hidden Indians. It was not until Braddock himself was shot in the back that the British broke in retreat, carrying off the body of their commanding officer.[1]

This article first appeared in *Military Review* (September–October 2001).

Asymmetric Warfare: Yesterday and Tomorrow

Why do I begin a discussion of tomorrow's conflicts with an account of a battle fought two and a half centuries ago? As an avid student of history, I believe it is critically important for us to understand that asymmetric warfare is not something new. In fact, it has been a recurring theme of American military history and is familiar to many of today's military officers. Many of its best historical examples come from the series of conflicts we refer to collectively as the Indian Wars. Braddock's defeat highlights as many useful insights as contemporary examples of asymmetric action, like Russian battles with the Chechens. Overcoming future challenges will require that we both understand the lessons from the past and develop strategies and tactics appropriate to tomorrow's battlefield.

While asymmetric warfare is not something new, it is very much in vogue today in the aftermath of the Persian Gulf War. Given America's resounding success in that conflict, potential adversaries have learned Iraq's lesson that it is foolish to try to match us conventionally. Instead, they are seeking ways to turn our strengths against us. This is the heart of the concept of asymmetry, broadly defined by Steven Metz and Douglas Johnson of the U.S. Army War College: "In the realm of military affairs and national security, asymmetry is acting, organizing, and thinking differently than opponents in order to maximize one's own advantages, exploit an opponent's weaknesses, attain the initiative, or gain greater freedom of action."[2]

Asymmetry on the Future Battlefield

In operational terms, asymmetry derives from one force deploying new capabilities that the opposing force does not perceive or understand, conventional capabilities that counter or overmatch the capabilities of its opponent, or capabilities that represent totally new methods of attack or defense—or a combination of these attributes.[3] The U.S. Army Training and Doctrine Command (TRADOC) now thinks of ways to characterize tomorrow's asymmetric challenges.[4] In considering its arguments, I was struck again by the utility of lessons learned from earlier campaigns against Native Americans such as Braddock's defeat. So I have matched TRADOC insights for the future with asymmetric examples from the past. Only by studying the lessons of history are we likely to adapt to asymmetric challenges.

The TRADOC analysis begins by stressing the differences between our current perception of the future operational environment and what is likely to be true. Today, we think of close combat as involving deliberate

actions conducted at a tempo decided by the United States and characterized by the application of technology and systems that leave opponents virtually helpless to respond or retaliate. Therefore, the public expects military
operations to involve few casualties and precision attacks, secure our homeland, and be short-lived. On the contrary, potential adversaries will likely
choose to fight in ways that negate these expectations. Future close combat
will be much more dynamic and lethal, marked by greater intensity, operational tempo, uncertainty, and psychological impact. We cannot expect the
experience of the Gulf War to be repeated.

Likely Characteristics of Adversaries

With this as a starting point, TRADOC has discussed attributes a potential enemy is likely to possess: greater knowledge of the physical conflict
environment, better situational awareness, a clearer understanding of U.S.
military forces, and an ability to adapt quickly to changing battlefield conditions. These attributes strongly mirror challenges for British, and later
American, soldiers in Indian campaigns of yesteryear.

The physical environment remains the defining variable of close
combat. For U.S. military forces, it is almost certain that future conflicts
will occur in regions where the enemy has a greater understanding of the
physical environment and has better optimized his forces to fight. A common characteristic of many Indian campaigns was the Indians' superior
knowledge of the terrain. A great example of this was the attack on the
forces of Colonel Henry Bouquet during his march to relieve Fort Pitt,
Pennsylvania, during Pontiac's War in August 1763. The Indians attacked
in an area of old growth forest, offering limited fields of fire, around Bushy
Run. They forced Bouquet's forces back into a defensive position on a hilltop, attacking the position repeatedly but without waiting for a counterattack. Their detailed knowledge of the area allowed them simply to fade
into the forest, suffering few casualties.[5] This is but one example of the advantages that accrued to many Indian tribes through the late 1800s.[6]

Opposing forces will also have greater situational awareness in future
conflicts. We should expect them to have human networks operating over
telephone lines or with cellular phones and using commercial imagery
systems. This will be critical, not only because the adversary can distribute
information quickly but also because crucial information will only be
available through human interaction. The United States, even with its
sophisticated intelligence, surveillance, and reconnaissance systems, will
have difficulty in complex settings unless it builds a more effective human

intelligence capability in strategically important regions. Moreover, these new adversaries will learn how to adapt not only technology but also tactics, formations, and operations in light of changing battlefield conditions during the course of operations. Such adaptations will help them counter a precision warfare strategy by creating uncertainty while also trying to control the nature and timing of combat engagements.

During the war in Chechnya, the Chechens fought using few prepared positions, preferring instead, as Chechen vice president Zelimkhan Yanderbaijev said, to "let the situation do the organizing."[7] They would move from city to city to deny Russian maneuver and fire superiority and would use the local population as cover for their activities.

Similarly, the Seminole Indians adapted continuously during the second Seminole War of 1835–1842. One noted historian puts it this way:

> The second Seminole War did not follow the precedent set in earlier Indian wars by producing a single dazzling stroke by a spectacularly brilliant leader. No fewer than seven American commanders would try and fail to bring the war to a successful conclusion. When confronted with superior firepower and at a tactical disadvantage, the Seminoles simply dispersed into small bands and continued to fight a guerrilla war...best suited to the terrain and their own temperament. Where other eastern Indians could usually be depended upon to follow the rules of the game—to defend a fixed position and be routed—the Seminoles...regularly rejected pitched battles and instead relied on ambushes and raids to bleed the Army, sap its strength, and generally discourage its leadership.[8]

In the future, such an adaptive enemy would put additional pressure on U.S. ability to respond, as their battlefield successes would be covered instantly by the global media, instantaneous communications, and media coverage.

Finally, our future adversaries will almost certainly have greater knowledge of U.S. forces than we will of theirs. We are the most studied military in the world. Foreign states have regular military features and, in some cases, entire journals (most notably Russia's *Foreign Military Review*) devoted to the assessment of U.S. military force structure, doctrine, operational concepts, and capabilities. All major U.S. Army field manuals (FMs) and joint doctrinal publications are freely available on the Internet, and many foreign organizations access them regularly. As an example, in April 2001 alone, the Center for Army Lessons Learned recorded 5,464 sessions on its Web site from Europe and 2,015 from Asia. This access, combined with their knowledge of battlefield terrain, greater situational awareness, and adaptability, will make future adversaries far more menacing.

How Will They Fight?

The essence of future asymmetric warfare is that adversaries will seek to offset our air, intelligence, surveillance, reconnaissance, and other technological advantages by fighting during periods of reduced visibility and in complex terrain and urban environments where they can gain sanctuary from U.S. strikes. This will also deny these areas and their inherent protective characteristics to U.S. forces, keeping us exposed and on the defensive.

U.S. forces will have to contend with greater uncertainty in the field as adversaries mask the size, location, disposition, and intentions of their forces. They will seek to convince U.S. commanders that they are using conventional tactics while making us vulnerable to unconventional, adaptive, and asymmetrical actions.

At the same time, adversaries will use both old and new technologies to great effect on the battlefield. They may use older technologies in unique ways, as the Chechens did by buying commercial scanners and radios to intercept Russian communications. They will also try to acquire advanced niche technologies like global positioning system jammers and systems for electronic attack to degrade our precision-strike capabilities significantly. Moreover, we must be prepared for adversaries to upgrade software capabilities in the middle of an operation, potentially allowing for a more networked opposition.

While some of the technology may be new, the Indian campaigns again provide useful insights. Many Indian campaigns demonstrated the effectiveness of asymmetric tactics in countering larger and better-armed British and American forces. In fact, "Indian skulking tactics—concealment and surprise, moving fire, envelopment and, when the enemy's ranks were broken, hand-to-hand combat—remained the cardinal features of Native American warfare" over a period of 140 years.[9] The longevity of their effectiveness shows how important it is to develop appropriate responses to asymmetric tactics.

One of the most successful Indian tactics was the ambush. Captain William Fetterman's massacre in 1866 near the Lodge Trail Ridge in Wyoming left 92 American soldiers dead in a classic ambush some believe was masterminded by Sioux leader Crazy Horse. A lesser-known battle, almost a century before, shows the effectiveness of the ambush, particularly when matched with reckless leadership. At the Battle of Blue Licks in August

1782, a group of 182 Kentucky militiamen, led by Colonel John Todd and including Daniel Boone and members of his family, was in hot pursuit of Indians who had attacked an American fort. Boone noticed the Indians were concealing their numbers by sharing tracks, yet making the trail easy to follow. He smelled an ambush by a force he estimated at 500 and advised breaking off the pursuit until reinforcements could arrive. A more junior officer yelled, "Them that ain't cowards follow me," and recklessly charged across the river toward several decoy Indians, with much of the force following him. The remaining Indians were waiting in ambush, as Boone had feared, and delivered a devastating defeat to the rangers.[10]

Like Blue Licks, the Battle of Bushy Run not only shows the efficacy of Indian raids until defeated by Bouquet's brilliant feigned retreat and flanking maneuvers; it also shows how an enemy can use deception effectively. The official history of Bushy Run says Bouquet's forces were engaged and surrounded by Indian forces at least equal in size to his own. However, when I toured the battlefield, Indian recreators, who have studied the battle extensively from the Indian point of view, maintained that the Indians numbered no more than 90 and that the tactics they used in the forest made their numbers seem larger. This disparity is a good example of attempts to confuse conventional forces so that the size of the opposing force is impossible to discern.

Finally, the Indian campaigns provide some excellent examples of the role of technological advances in asymmetric campaigns. Noted historian Armstrong Starkey emphasizes that the Europeans arrived in North America during a time of military revolution in Europe:

> European soldiers brought the new weapons and techniques of this revolution with them to North America and by 1675 had provoked a military revolution of a sort among Native Americans, a revolution that for 140 years gave them a tactical advantage over their more numerous and wealthier opponents.[11]

Specifically, King Philip's War (1675–1676) was the first conflict in which the Indians had modern flintlock firearms. This proved an important advantage because some of the American militias were only equipped with matchlocks and pikes and because the Indians were excellent marksmen.[12] More than 200 years after the Civil War, the same faulty assumptions were still at work—namely, that the U.S. military retained unmatched technical advantages over its more primitive adversaries. At that time, the U.S. Government rearmed its forces with breechloaders in place of magazine rifles—due to a bias against unaimed shots and excessive use of ammunition—while the Plains Indians acquired such weapons by direct purchase and thus, in some cases, had superior arms in the 1870s. We must be on the lookout for technological matches like these in our own future conflicts.

New Threats

We have seen the great utility of examining historical conflicts between Europeans and Native Americans to learn lessons about possible future conflict. Yet there are two additional dimensions to asymmetric warfare that must be mentioned—the threat of weapons of mass destruction, potentially used against the American homeland, and of cyberattacks on U.S. military, government, and private information systems.

At the heart of asymmetry is the assumption that an adversary will choose to attack the weakest point. In the case of the United States, asymmetric tools may well entail terrorist acts—with or without nuclear, biological, or chemical weapons—on the U.S. homeland designed to disrupt deployments, limit access, erode public support, and take the fight to the American people. In some respects, this homeland tactic is not new. Beginning with King Philip's War, the New England Indians abandoned their traditional restraints and "prepared to wage total war on all of the colonists, making no distinction between combatant and non-combatant."[13] Attacks on Americans using weapons of mass destruction take these homeland tactics to a new level. Because of the devastation of these attacks and the interest of many potential adversaries in acquiring these capabilities, the United States must develop strategies for preventing and responding to such an occurrence.

The cyberthreat now facing the United States is equally compelling and risks both the effectiveness of U.S. forces on the battlefield and the safety of private and government systems throughout the United States. Recent Joint Chiefs of Staff–directed cyberwarfare exercises such as ELIGIBLE RECEIVER and ZENITH STAR showed how vulnerable command and control networks are to cyberattacks, a prime asymmetric target given the continued U.S. military reliance on information technology. Moreover, there are now approximately 30 nations that have developed "aggressive computer-warfare programs."[14]

Again, there is a relevant Indian war complement to today's challenges. Indians of the Southern Plains disrupted American efforts in the West through unconventional means:

The telegraph line, which once had commanded their awe, no longer was mysterious. By 1882, the Apache had learned its function and its method of operation. When they jumped the reservation, they would cut the lines and remove long sections of wire, or they would remove a short piece of wire and replace it with a thin strip of rawhide, so cleverly splicing the two together that the line would appear intact and the location of the break could take days of careful checking to discover.[15]

This disruption foreshadows the potentially far greater problems from cyberattacks if we do not design strategy and tactics for dealing with this as part of an asymmetric campaign.

Preparing for Asymmetric Attacks

The first step in preparing to better meet tomorrow's challenges is to learn from the past. As the examples drawn here indicate, there is a rich history to be tapped in the early American experience. But there are many other examples as well—Yugoslav partisans fighting the occupying Nazis or Afghans against the Russians and Serbs in the recent North Atlantic Treaty Organization operation in Kosovo. Military commanders must study history. Modern, technologically sophisticated warfare—with the asymmetric challenges that accompany it—makes that requirement more true, not less.

Our forces must also be adaptive. Just as our adversaries will continuously change tactics and approaches to seek our weaknesses, so must we be able to counter them through continuous adaptation. If we do not, we risk the mistakes of the past. "While European military revolutions provided states with the means to project power into the interior of North America, they did not provide troops with appropriate training and tactics to succeed on the frontier."[16] Therefore, our forces, doctrine, and tactics must continue to embrace agility and adaptability and prepare for a range of missions. The Army continues to do so in its most recent doctrinal publications, FM 1 and FM 3–0.[17] Efforts to address asymmetric threats must also retain the unique American strengths—superior training, leadership, and technology—that give us an edge against any potential adversary.

Finally, we must guard against arrogance. An account at the time of Braddock's defeat noted the irony that his preparations for the march to Fort Duquesne were precise. He attended to every minute detail except "the one that mattered most: Indian affairs."[18] He dismissed those Ohio Indian chiefs who might have been allies for his expedition as savages who could not possibly assist disciplined troops. We must not fall into the same trap of underestimating a potential adversary because of his different culture or seemingly inferior capability. To do so would be to repeat the errors of the past with potentially devastating future consequences.

Notes

[1] Fred Anderson, *Crucible of War: The Seven Years' War and the Fate of Empire in British North America, 1754–1766* (New York: Alfred A. Knopf, 2000), 94–107.

[2] Steven Metz and Douglas V. Johnson II, *Asymmetry and U.S. Military Strategy: Definition, Background, and Strategic Concepts* (Carlisle, PA: Strategic Studies Institute, U.S. Army War College, January 2001), 5.

[3] This operational definition of asymmetry is drawn from my conversations with General Montgomery C. Meigs, Commander of U.S. Army Forces, Europe, who is an excellent source for insights on operational art.

[4] I am deeply indebted to General John Abrams and his staff, especially Colonel Maxie MacFarland at TRADOC, for many of the ideas presented here. In addition, I would like to thank Professors Graham Turbiville and William Robertson at Fort Leavenworth, Kansas, for their assistance with the historical examples. Their help was invaluable in constructing this chapter. I am also grateful to Erin Conaton, professional staff member with the House of Representatives' Committee on Armed Services, for her assistance with researching and writing this chapter.

[5] Anderson, 547–563.

[6] Jack C. Lane's *Armed Progressive: General Leonard Wood* (San Rafael, CA: Presidio Press, 1978) notes that as a new surgeon in the Army Medical Department, Wood

> learned why the Apaches . . . proved to be the army's most impervious foe in the 1870s and 1880s. Perfecting guerrilla warfare to a fine art, the Apaches operated in small raiding parties rarely numbering more than 100 braves. The hardy warriors had developed incredible stamina and a seemingly unlimited ability to endure with only the bare necessities for long periods in the almost impenetrable, barren mountains and deserts of southern Arizona and northern Mexico. Organizing themselves into small bands, they roamed the Arizona territory at will until, pursued closely by the army, they retired into the strongholds of the Sierra Madre Mountains. To defeat such an enemy required exceptional leaders and men.

[7] "Chechen Commander on Modern Separatism," *Nezavisimoye Voyennoye Obozreniye* (January 22–28, 1999), 2.

[8] John D. Waghelstein, "The Second Seminole War: Lessons Learned, Relearned and Unlearned," *Low Intensity Conflict and Law Enforcement* (Winter 1992), 4.

[9] Armstrong Starkey, *European and Native American Warfare, 1675–1815* (Norman, OK: University of Oklahoma Press, 1998), 167.

[10] Isaac Newton Skelton III and Earl Franklin Skelton, *Ike, This Is You* (Washington, DC: 1995), 132–141. The author's great-great-great grandfather, Squire Boone, was wounded during this battle.

[11] Starkey, viii.

[12] Ibid., 71–72.

[13] Ibid., 72.

[14] James Adams, "Virtual Defense," *Foreign Affairs* (May/June 2001), 102.

[15] Odie B. Faulk, *The Geronimo Campaign* (New York: Oxford University Press, 1969), 46.

[16] Starkey, 169.

[17] U.S. Army FM 1, *The Army* (Washington, DC: U.S. Government Printing Office, June 2001); FM 3–0, *Operations* (Washington, DC: U.S. Government Printing Office, June 2001).

[18] "The Journal of Captain Robert Chomley's Batman," May 20 and 23, 1755, cited in Anderson, 94. The rest of the account of Braddock's defeat is largely drawn from Anderson, 94–107.

Chapter 12

You're Not From Around Here, Are You?

Know thy enemy. That adage has been repeated since armies first clashed on the field of battle. Understanding enemy intentions, tactics, and vulnerabilities is an essential part of warfare. But it is also necessary to know your friends. Making enemies is easy, but it is harder to acquire friends. The wrong approach to allied or occupied countries can quickly create enemies.

The United States has not been an occupying power since the period immediately following World War II. In Korea and Vietnam, where the goal was fighting and leaving, sensitivity to local culture was important, although it was not a long-term concern. In Iraq, however, a cultural divide brought to the fore issues that three generations of soldiers have considered only peripherally.

Operating in a foreign land can be a minefield. Few members of the Armed Forces will be familiar with cultural traditions of the countries in which they operate. Yet violation of local norms and beliefs can turn a welcoming population into vocal enemies.

Iraqis arrested by U.S. troops have had their heads forced to the ground, a position forbidden by Islam except during prayers. This action offends detainees as well as bystanders. In Bosnia, American soldiers angered Serbs by greeting them with the two-fingered peace sign, a gesture commonly used by their Croat enemies. And the circled-finger "A–OK" signal was a gross insult to Somalis. The military has enough to worry about without alienating the local population.

U.S. Representative Jim Cooper (D–TN) co-authored this article, which will be published in *Joint Force Quarterly* (Issue 36, forthcoming).

Afghanistan and Iraq

Though it may be premature to draw definitive lessons from Afghanistan or Iraq, it is clear that the Armed Forces lack sophisticated knowledge of foreign countries. That does not dishonor their performance; cultural awareness is not a mission-essential task—but it should be.

Winning a conflict means more than subduing an enemy. While the U.S. military ran into trouble in the past, it was not because it lacked combat skills, personal courage, or the necessary resources. As operations in Afghanistan and Iraq have demonstrated, the process of restructuring the political order, economy, and social well being of an entire country is as critical as defeating organized resistance. But it is cultural awareness that helps determine whether a host population supports long-term American military presence—and may determine the outcome of the mission.

It is uncertain whether the majority of the Iraqi people will support the multinational efforts, which many see as responsible for the unrest. Rebuilding Iraq may hinge on drawing appropriate inferences from ethnic and religious aspects of its culture—including tribal dynamics—and then properly responding to them. Commanders in Iraq have stressed the importance of being aware of these elements of the security landscape.

The House Armed Services Committee held a hearing in late 2003 to examine the lessons of Operation *Iraqi Freedom* at which Major General Robert Scales, Jr., USA (Ret.), highlighted the requirement for cultural awareness among both civilian and military personnel. His testimony emphasized that had American planners better understood Iraqi culture, efforts to win the peace would have been more sound. Senior officials and commanders might have reached a different conclusion on the willingness of Iraqis to welcome the U.S. military for an extended period of reconstruction.

Events during Operation *Uphold Democracy* in Haiti further emphasized cultural differences:

> The Army in general had little appreciation of Haitian history and culture. Few planners knew anything about Haiti other than its basic geography. In a combat operation, where overwhelming firepower achieves objectives, sensitivity for the local population's culture and traditions clearly is not a top priority. In a peace operation such as *Uphold Democracy*, however, knowledge of how a people think and act, and how they might react to military intervention, arguably becomes paramount. The U.S. military culture in general focuses on

training warriors to use fire and maneuver and tends to resist the notion of culture awareness.[1]

The need for cultural awareness is not unique to the American military. Russian soldiers in Chechnya made cultural blunders in dealing with local civilians who, once insulted or mistreated, either supported active resistance fighters or joined them. Moreover, Russian leaders realized that they had underestimated the influence of religion in the region.

Cultural Awareness

Understanding the culture and social factors unique to the countries in which Americans are most likely to be deployed will make the environment work to their advantage. On the lowest level, cultural awareness means knowing enough about local culture to permit military personnel to operate effectively. Along with linguistic capability, cultural awareness can highlight political, social, and other characteristics of the operational area. It can explain why local people may see things differently from Americans. It can enable troops on the ground to understand how their attitudes and actions directly influence mission success or failure.

The Armed Forces often operate as members of coalitions and alliances. Nations cannot work together without recognizing their cultural differences—where the other guy is coming from. That awareness becomes even more important over time. It is not a touchy-feely or nice-to-have social grace; it is basic intelligence on attitudes and potential actions of host nations and coalition partners. Only such insights can enable the military to understand other cultures.

The Marine Corps' 1940 manual on insurgency noted that:

> The motive in small wars is not material destruction. It is usually a project dealing with social, economic, and political development of the people. It is of primary importance that the fullest benefit be derived from the psychological aspects of the situation. That implies a serious study of the people, their racial, political, religious, and mental development. By analysis and study the reasons for the existing emergency may be deduced; the most practical method of solving the problem is to understand the possible approaches thereto and the repercussion to be expected from any actions which may be contemplated. By this study and ability to apply correct psychological doctrine, many pitfalls may be avoided and the success of the undertaking assured.[2]

Stability operations and postconflict reconstruction are among the major challenges facing the military in the post–Cold War world. This was clear even before Afghanistan and Iraq—two battlefronts in the global war on terrorism.

The Army and Marine Corps have a history of conducting such operations under the rubric of *low-intensity conflict* and *military operations other than war.* Operations in the Philippines from 1899 to 1903 and in Haiti from 1994 to 1995 also offer examples of partial success in such efforts. Other than foreign area officers, defense attachés, and Special Forces, there is insufficient cultural awareness and linguistic skill among commissioned and noncommissioned officers.

A combat brigade would not be deployed into hostile territory without maps. The beliefs of a culture are as critical as terrain features. The unit should have the cultural coordinates as well as the geographical ones.

Defining the Need

Predeployment preparations must include cultural awareness training. Just as personnel are trained in specific tactics, they should be provided an understanding of the environment where they will operate. The ability of deployed personnel to draw inferences from experience or study could contribute decisively to the national strategy.

Scales describes the operational environment and importance of cultural awareness:

> The image of sergeants and captains acting alone in the Afghanistan wilderness and the sands of Iraq, innovating on the fly with instruments of strategic killing power, reaffirms the truth that today's leaders must acquire the skills and wisdom to lead indirectly at a much lower level. Today's tactical leaders must be able to act alone in ambiguous and uncertain circumstances, lead soldiers they cannot touch, think so as to anticipate the enemy's actions—they must be tactically proactive rather than reactive.[3]

The need for cultural awareness extends beyond the foxhole. Senior officers must create an appropriate command climate. Civilian officials need to be culturally aware in developing policy and strategy. They must know that imposing American values on unwilling people in a foreign country may have undesired strategic and operational consequences. Deployed personnel must have sufficient awareness in theaters where ambiguous and contradictory situations are the norm. And because of the reliance on the Reserve components, they must have similar training.

At a minimum, training on cultural awareness should occur on two levels. The first would be focused on planners. As an interim measure, programs for flag and field grade officers would be appropriate, along with greater emphasis on cultural awareness in curricula at both the staff and war college level. As soon as practical, that training should be extended to all officers.

One report on the experiences of general officers who served in Bosnia, Somalia, and Haiti noted the need for additional training:

> Greater emphasis must be placed on geopolitical and cultural training for the Army's officer corps. Such training must begin at the officer basic course and continue at all levels of professional military education. Officers at all grades will benefit from such training because of the likelihood that they will be involved in peace operations on multiple occasions throughout their careers.[4]

Training should be comprehensive and offered to both the Active and Reserve components. The ideal program would reward continued learning and require that officers get an early start on becoming indirect leaders. Unit leaders would mentor their performance while undergoing instruction. Both the classroom and distance learning would stretch across career assignments. The curriculum would be historically based and thoroughly joint in nature.

The second tier involves language and area studies. Commissioned and noncommissioned leaders must possess some language skills and understanding of nations to which they are deployed. This sort of training results in street sense—knowing how to gather intelligence from local people. That can only happen with cultural awareness. It is the level on which simple linguistic skills are essential: "Halt, lay down your weapon." But it is better to warn of the likely consequences of such interactions with locals.

Compared to education, training involves imparting specific skills. It can be prepackaged and offered throughout a career. It is part of the daily military routine. As one officer described his experience in Bosnia:

> Specialists are assigned to ensure the commanders are politically astute, historically aware, and culturally sensitized. Unfortunately, this information has no real conduit down to company and platoon levels, and perhaps most important, to the individual soldier. In most organizations of the conventional infantry force, there is no foreign area officer or civil affairs officer who specializes in these matters to fill the gap. Although it is vital for senior leaders to be well informed in these facets of operations, it is often the company commander, platoon

leader, or squad leader who finds himself . . . dealing with the civilian populace day by day.[5]

A Matter of Timing

Cultural awareness must be taught on the primary level. And knowing your enemy should be accompanied by knowing your friends. Moreover, educational and training programs should be focused on those regions likely to pose threats to national security as well as cultures vital to long-term strategic relationships.

Mandating cultural awareness training may appear a simple requirement, but implementing it is a daunting task. First, identifying which cultures to study and what level of proficiency to attain is demanding. There is no one-size-fits-all answer to cultural awareness. Nonspecific theories on cultural contexts can be detrimental, and generalizing cultural characteristics can be deceptive:

> Americans are often direct in their conversations, expecting the truth with no hint of deception. At the same time, Americans also tend to be uncomfortable with silent moments. People in some other countries, though, may prefer not to be direct and may shift their eyes away from the American. . . . a person who is reluctant to maintain eye contact is called shifty-eyed and arouses suspicion. But in some countries an attempt to maintain eye contact may be perceived as a sign of aggression. Accordingly, in Japan, South Korea, Taiwan, and other Asian countries, maintaining eye contact is not an acceptable behavior. On the other hand, in Saudi Arabia, eye contact and gestures of openness are important and could facilitate communications.[6]

Predeployment training focuses on the current military situation for all the obvious reasons. But cultural awareness training must be accomplished on a regular basis and well in advance. Thus, that knowledge must already be in place before it is time to go.

The national security strategy envisions a more assertively expeditionary military. Over the last two decades, extended coalition operations have become the norm. This requires operational planning that recognizes the importance of cultural awareness. If implemented, integrated training to develop such awareness will have lasting, positive effects for plans, actionable intelligence, and the credibility of U.S. objectives. Experience teaches that cultural awareness is a force multiplier. It is time to be serious about enhancing our knowledge of today's world. The Armed Forces are busier than ever before, but they are not too busy to be culturally aware.

Notes

[1] Walter B. Kretchik, Robert F. Baumann, and John T. Fishel, *Invasion, Intervention, Intervasion: A Concise History of the U.S. Army Operation* Uphold Democracy (Fort Leavenworth, KS: U.S. Army Command and General Staff College, 1998), 188.

[2] U.S. Marine Corps, *Small Wars Manual* (Washington, DC: U.S. Government Printing Office, 1940), 18.

[3] Major General Robert H. Scales, Jr., USA (Ret.), letter to the Honorable Ike Skelton, June 12, 2003.

[4] U.S. Institute for Peace, *Alternative National Military Strategies for the United States* (Carlisle Barracks, PA: Strategic Studies Institute, U.S. Army War College, 2000), 6.

[5] Joel B. Krauss, "Cultural Awareness in Stability and Support Operations," *Infantry* 89, no. 1 (January/April 1999), 15.

[6] Gary Bonvillian and William A. Nowlin, "Cultural Awareness: An Essential Element of Doing Business Abroad," *Business Horizons* 37, no. 6 (November/December 1994), 45.

Recommended Reading for Military Professionals

Ambrose, Stephen E. *Undaunted Courage: Meriwether Lewis, Thomas Jefferson, and the Opening of the American West*. New York: Simon and Schuster, 1996.

Ambrose augments information from the journals of both Lewis and Clark with his personal travels along their route in this biography of Lewis. He chronicles the events of the "Corps of Discovery" and assesses their military leadership and negotiations with various native people.

———. *The Victors: Eisenhower and His Boys: The Men of World War II*. Rockland, MA: Wheeler Publishers, 1999.

This book draws heavily from Ambrose's biography of General Dwight D. Eisenhower and several military histories that recount the Allied push across the European continent in 1944–1945 from the frontline trooper's perspective.

Anderson, Fred. *Crucible of War: The Seven Years' War and the Fate of Empire in British North America, 1754–1766*. New York: Alfred A. Knopf, 2000.

Anderson revisits the role that the Seven Years' War played in the American Revolution. He argues that the war was not merely a backdrop to the Revolution but rather a critical event that forged the tensions leading to the disintegration of the British Empire in America.

Bamm, Peter. *Alexander the Great*. New York: McGraw-Hill, 1968.

As a ruler who both inherited power from his father Philip and acquired power by conquest, Alexander practiced tolerance and restraint in an attempt to invest his sovereignty over Persia with the character of legitimacy.

Bonaparte, Napoleon. *The Military Maxims of Napoleon*. Edited by William E. Cairnes and David G. Chandler. New York: Da Capo Press, 1995.

This is a distillation of the knowledge, intuition, and wisdom of history's greatest military commander. Napoleon's thought, theories, and commentaries on war are presented in the form of accessible and readable maxims with explanatory comments.

Brownlee, Richard S. *Gray Ghosts of the Confederacy: Guerrilla Warfare in the West, 1862–1867*. Baton Rouge: Louisiana State University Press, 1958.

This history of the Confederate guerrilla warfare in the west from 1862 to 1867 filled a gap in the scholarship on the Civil War. As early as 1862, the guerrillas dominated Missouri to such an extent that the Union Army stationed 60,000 troops in the state to try to control the violence—troops that could have served a better purpose if stationed elsewhere.

Clausewitz, Carl von. *On War*. Edited and translated by Peter Paret and Michael Eliot Howard. Princeton: Princeton University Press, 1984.

This is the most significant attempt in Western history to understand war, both in its internal dynamics and as an instrument of policy. Since its first appearance in 1832, this book has been read throughout the world and has stimulated generations of soldiers, statesmen, and intellectuals.

Cohen, Eliot A. *Supreme Command: Soldiers, Statesmen, and Leadership in Wartime*. New York: Anchor Books, 2003.

Cohen examines the strategies of Abraham Lincoln, Georges Clemenceau, Winston Churchill, and David Ben Gurion and addresses broader questions about the tension between politicians and generals in a wartime democracy. He argues that these men were great wartime heads of state because they were able to finesse a relationship with their military leaders that kept the balance of power squarely in (their own) civilian hands.

Connell, Evan S. *Son of the Morning Star: Custer and the Little Big Horn*. San Francisco: North Point Press, 1997.

Connell's examination of the Little Big Horn is generally considered to be the most reliable account of the subject. He makes good use of his meticulous research and novelist's eye for the story and detail to recreate the heroism, foolishness, and savagery of this crucial chapter in the history of the West.

The Constitution of the United States of America. Bedford, MA: Applewood Books, 1995.

The founding document of American government is printed in its entirety without notes or commentary.

Coram, Robert. *Boyd: The Fighter Pilot Who Changed the Art of War*. Boston: Little, Brown and Company, 2002.

This is a deeply researched and detailed biography of John Boyd, a crackerjack jet fighter pilot, a visionary scholar, and an innovative military strategist. He wrote the first manual on jet aerial combat, was primarily responsible for designing the F–15 and the F–16 jet fighters, was a leading voice in the post–Vietnam War military reform movement, and shaped the successful U.S. military strategy in the Persian Gulf War.

Creasy, Edward Shepherd. *Fifteen Decisive Battles of the World: From Marathon to Waterloo*. New York: Da Capo Press, 1994.

This book, first published in 1851, is a classic account of famous battles of the past 2,300 years that fundamentally changed the course of world history. Battles under discussion include the battle of Marathon, the victory of Arminius over the Roman legions under Varus, the battle of Hastings, the defeat of the Spanish Armada, and the battle of Waterloo.

Cronin, Vincent. *Napoleon Bonaparte: An Intimate Biography*. New York: Harper Collins, 1990.

Cronin approached this book as a study of Napoleon's character, an attempt to "picture a living, breathing man." Toward this end, Cronin concentrates on events that throw light on Napoleon's character. Military campaigns are only outlined, although civil matters are dealt with in more depth.

DeBeer, Gavin Rylands. *Hannibal: Challenging Rome's Supremacy*. New York: Viking Press, 1969.

Acknowledging the difficulty presented by the absence of sympathetic primary sources about Hannibal—everything that is known about him came from or passed through the hands of his enemies, the Romans—deBeer has produced an account of the leader of Carthage and his role in preparing for the Second Punic War.

Eisenhower, John S.D. *Yanks: The Epic Story of the American Army in World War I*. New York: Free Press, 2002.

Eisenhower presents the U.S. involvement in the war from the perspective of statesmen and generals. He focuses primarily on senior officers, such as Douglas MacArthur, George Patton, and George C. Marshall, and lesser-known figures like Charles Summerall. Without denying the administrative problems and the casualties caused by inexperience and improvisation, Eisenhower stresses the high American learning curves at all levels.

Faragher, John Mack. *Daniel Boone: The Life and Legend of an American Pioneer*. New York: Owl Books, 1993.

Faragher reexamines the popular image of Daniel Boone and argues that he is worthy of attention as a personification of the westward movement rather than as an unlettered backwoodsman, skilled hunter, and Indian fighter.

Fehrenbach, T.R. *This Kind of War: The Classic Korean War History*. Washington, DC: Brassey's Inc., 1994.

In this book, originally published in 1963 as *This Kind of War: A Study in Unpreparedness*, Fehrenbach presents a broad view of events in the Korean and international arenas and offers sharp insight into the successes and failures of U.S. forces. Partly drawn from official records, operations journals, and histories, it is based largely on the personal narratives of the small-unit commanders and their troops.

Frank, Richard B. *Guadalcanal: The Definitive Account of the Landmark Battle*. New York: Penguin, 1992.

New translations of Japanese accounts, recently declassified documents, and strategies and tactics of both sides inform this record of America's first major offensive of the Pacific war. Frank evaluates the adversaries' strengths and weaknesses, stressing in particular the shortcomings of the U.S. Navy and the Japanese Army. He argues convincingly that Guadalcanal was the turning point in the Pacific.

Freeman, Douglas Southall. *Lee.* New York: Scribner, 1997.

> This reissue of Richard Harwell's 1961 abridgement of Freeman's 1935 Pulitzer Prize–winning *R.E. Lee* chronicles all the major aspects and highlights of Lee's military career and includes a new introduction by James McPherson.

Freeman, Douglas Southall, William J. Jacobs, and Richard Barksdale Harwell. *Washington: An Abridgement in One Volume by Richard Harwell of the Seven-Volume George Washington by Douglas Southall Freeman.* New York: Charles Scribner's Sons, 1968.

> This abridged text of Freeman's Pulitzer Prize–winning biography of Washington provides a much more easily read summary of Washington's life than the original series.

Freidel, Frank B. *Franklin D. Roosevelt: A Rendezvous with Destiny.* Boston: Little, Brown and Company, 1990.

> Freidel, whose four-volume biography of the young FDR concluded with the launching of the New Deal, offers a one-volume complete biography. It concentrates on Roosevelt's Presidency, with public events the consistent focus, and the private man left mainly alone.

Grant, Ulysses S. *Personal Memoirs: Ulysses S. Grant.* New York: Modern Library, 1999.

> Destitute and wracked by throat cancer, Grant finished writing his memoirs shortly before his death in 1885. Today their clear prose stands as a model of autobiography and is probably the best piece of writing produced by a participant in the War Between the States. Apart from Lincoln, no man deserves more credit for securing the Northern victory than Grant, and this chronicle of campaigns and battles tells how he did it.

Handel, Michael I. *Masters of War: Classical Strategic Thought.* New York: Frank Cass and Company, 2000.

> This study is based on a detailed textual analysis of the classical works on war by Clausewitz, Sun Tzu, Mao Tse-tung, Jomini, and Machiavelli. The central conclusion is that the logic of waging war and of strategic thinking is as universal and timeless as human nature itself.

Hibbert, Christopher. *Nelson: A Personal History*. New York: Da Capo Press, 1996.

In this tale of Nelson's life on and off the high seas, Hibbert illuminates the admiral's personality, his personal and political friendships, his relationship with Sir William Hamilton, and his passionate love affair with Hamilton's wife. Whether quarreling with royalty, wooing beautiful women around the world, or winning history's most famous sea battles, Hibbert's irascible Nelson is a character for all times.

Holm, Jeanne M. *Women in the Military: An Unfinished Revolution*. Novato, CA: Presidio Press, 1992.

Holm has updated this standard work, originally published in 1982, with material on the role of military women in the Grenada, Panama, and Persian Gulf campaigns, along with a discussion of the ongoing debate over the combat exclusion laws and draft policies relating to women.

Homan, Lynn M., and Thomas Reilly. *Black Knights: The Story of the Tuskegee Airmen*. Gretna, LA: Pelican Publishing Company, 2001.

Through interviews with Tuskegee airmen and their families, as well as archival research, Homan and Reilly convey the organizational and personal struggles behind the Tuskegee experience. They detail the training and war missions of the black airmen and the hardships overcome in Europe as well as at home.

Houlahan, Thomas G. *Gulf War: The Complete History*. New London, NH: Schrenker Military Publishing, 1999.

Using published Gulf War narratives and interviews with commanders, Houlahan has assembled a narrative of every Coalition maneuver battalion through the war in an attempt to close the gap between the reality of the war and the public perception of it.

Hubbard, Elbert. *A Message to Garcia*. Mount Vernon, NY: Peter Pauper Press, 1983.

This short essay, set against the backdrop of the Spanish-American War, has been translated into every major language and is the fifth most widely distributed book in history. Military and business leaders alike have applied its theme—that a hero is a man who does his job—to their endeavors.

Jenkins, Roy. *Churchill: A Biography*. New York: Farrar Straus Giroux, 2001.

Jenkins' mastery of British political history and his tenure as a member of Parliament enrich this book, which adds much to the vast library of works on Churchill. While acknowledging his subject's prickly nature, Jenkins credits Churchill for, among other things, recognizing far earlier than his peers the dangers of Hitler's regime. He praises Churchill for his leadership during the war years, especially at the outset, when England stood alone and in imminent danger of defeat. He also examines Churchill's struggle to forge political consensus to meet that crisis, and he sheds new light on Churchill's postwar decline.

Kaplan, Robert D. *Warrior Politics: Why Leadership Demands a Pagan Ethos*. New York: Random House, 2001.

Kaplan extracts historical models and rationales from the works of Machiavelli, Malthus, Hobbes, and others to advocate a foreign policy based on the morality of results rather than good intentions. From these classics, he draws examples of exploiting military might, stealth, cunning, and what he dubs "anxious foresight" in order to lead, fight, and defeat adversaries who challenge the prevailing balance of power.

Keegan, John, ed. *The Book of War*. New York: Viking Press, 1999.

In this anthology of war writings, Keegan has collected some of the best that has been thought and said about armed conflict over the course of 25 centuries, beginning with Thucydides and concluding with a British soldier's comments about the 1991 Gulf War.

———. *The Face of Battle*. New York: Viking Press, 1976.

Keegan creates a realistic picture of the fears, pressures, and mechanics of fighting a battle, using Agincourt, Waterloo, and the Somme as examples.

———. *The Price of Admiralty: The Evolution of Naval Warfare*. New York: Penguin USA, 1990.

Keegan explores the changing nature of war at sea by dissecting four crucial sea battles, each featuring a different type of warship: Trafalgar (wooden sailing ships), Jutland (ironclad dreadnoughts), Midway (aircraft carriers), and the Battle of the Atlantic (submarines). He focuses on how technology, tactics, strategy, and training influenced combat operations in the battles.

MacArthur, Douglas. *Reminiscences*. Annapolis, MD: United States Naval Institute, 2001.

MacArthur's supporters believe his genius for command and ability to implement that command by strategy stand as landmarks in military history. His critics are not so kind, calling him a gigantic ego paying homage to himself in this book. This self-portrait is a moving final testament to a life of service that began at West Point and continued in Vera Cruz during the Mexican uprisings and throughout the world wars. Appointed Supreme Commander of Allied Forces in the Pacific, MacArthur was the architect of the campaign to drive the Japanese from their strongholds at Bataan, Corregidor, and New Guinea. Although the autobiography was written more than 30 years ago, it continues to be a valuable document of the period.

McCullough, David G. *Truman*. New York: Simon and Schuster, 1992.

In this 1993 Pulitzer Prize–winning biography, McCullough evaluates Truman's Presidency and argues that history has validated most of his wartime and Cold War decisions. McCullough also devotes considerable attention to defining Truman's character and portraying him as not only a President, but also a man.

McPherson, James M. *Battle Cry of Freedom: The Civil War Era*. Oxford: Oxford University Press, 2003.

Published in 1988 to universal acclaim, this single-volume treatment of the Civil War quickly became recognized as the new standard in its field. McPherson combines a brisk writing style with an admirable thoroughness. He covers the military aspects of the war in all of the necessary detail, and also provides a helpful framework describing the complex economic, political, and social forces behind the conflict.

Millet, Alan R. and Williamson Murray. *A War to Be Won*. Cambridge: Harvard University Press, 2000.

The authors examine the Second World War from the operational level, detailing strategy and tactics. They also discuss weapons development and production, as well as intelligence and deception, including mistakes and successes on both sides.

Moore, Harold G., and Joseph L. Galloway. *We Were Soldiers Once... and Young: Ia Drang—The Battle That Changed the War in Vietnam.* New York: Random House, 1992.

This book combines the memories of Moore, who commanded the 1st Battalion, 7th Cavalry, and Galloway, the only reporter present during the 34-day battle against the Viet Cong at Ia Drang, with more than 100 in-depth interviews with survivors on both sides. The authors present Ia Drang as an archetype of a self-defeating U.S. strategy that emphasized wearing down a determined and skillful enemy on the battlefield. The result was an unacceptably high level of American losses for the results achieved.

Morris, Donald R. *The Washing of the Spears: The Rise and Fall of the Zulu Nation.* New York: Da Capo Press, 1998.

Filled with colorful characters, dramatic battles like Isandhlwana and Rorke's Drift, and an inexorable narrative momentum, this unsurpassed history details the 60-year existence of the world's mightiest African empire—from its brutal formation and zenith under the military genius Shaka (1787–1828), through its inevitable collision with white expansionism, to its dissolution under Cetshwayo in the Zulu War of 1879.

Murtha, John P., and John Plashal. *From Vietnam to 9/11: On the Front Lines of National Security.* University Park, PA: Pennsylvania State University Press, 2003.

Murtha, the first Vietnam combat veteran elected to Congress, combines memories of his personal experiences with his analysis of failures and successes in American policymaking decisions about national security and foreign policy.

Prados, John. *Combined Fleet Decoded: The Secret History of American Intelligence and the Japanese Navy in World War II.* New York: Random House, 1995.

This ambitious work is not simply a rundown of code-breaking successes, but an astonishing demonstration of how the day-to-day accumulation of knowledge can produce extraordinary results. Its accounting of Japanese intelligence is unprecedented in detail. Its reassessment of battles and campaigns is presented not just in terms of troops or ships but in how the secret war actually played out.

Ricks, Thomas E. *Making the Corps.* New York: Scribners, 1997.

Ricks combines his account of following a platoon of young men through 11 weeks of Marine Corps boot camp with commentary on what separates the demanding, disciplined culture of America's military elite from the more permissive culture of its civilian society. Ricks also examines how the corps is dealing with such critical social and political issues as race relations, gender equality, and sexual orientation.

Scales, Robert H., Jr. *Yellow Smoke: The Future of Land Warfare for America's Military.* Lanham, MD: Rowman and Littlefield Publishers, 2003.

The author focuses on the land forces—the U.S. Army and U.S. Marine Corps—in this attempt to anticipate how changes in geopolitics, technology, and domestic politics will alter the character of future wars. He maintains that America's new age of warfare—"limited" wars fought for limited ends and with limited means—began with the Korean War and that lessons learned in each active conflict since help to clarify America's strategic direction and to codify a new and uniquely American way of fighting limited wars.

Shirer, William L. *The Rise and Fall of the Third Reich.* New York: Simon and Schuster, 1990.

Since its publication in 1960, this monumental study of Hitler's German Empire has been widely acclaimed as the definitive record of the blackest hours of the 20th century. Shirer's text offers an unparalleled and thrillingly told examination of how Adolf Hitler nearly succeeded in conquering the world. With millions of copies in print around the globe, it has attained the status of a vital and enduring classic.

Sides, Hampton. *Ghost Soldiers: The Forgotten Epic Story of World War II's Most Dramatic Mission.* New York: Doubleday, 2001.

Sides interviewed participants of the rescue of 500 American and Allied prisoners of war from Cabanatuan prison camp on the Philippine island of Luzon. This account intertwines the tale of these prisoners, who were survivors of the Bataan Death March in 1942, and 121 officers and men of the Army's Sixth Ranger Battalion.

Slim, William Joseph, Viscount. *Defeat Into Victory: Battling Japan in Burma and India, 1942–1945.* With a new introduction by David W. Hogan, Jr. New York: Cooper Square Press, 2000.

This is an updated version of the classic, definitive account of the Burma campaign in World War II. It presents the history of the victory against Japan in India by Field Marshal Slim, who led shattered British forces from Burma to India in one of the lesser-known but more nightmarish retreats of the war, and the ultimate liberation of India and Burma from the Japanese Army.

Sugden, John. *Tecumseh: A Life*. New York: Henry Holt and Company, 1999.

Over 30 years in the writing, this is the first authoritative biography of the principal organizer and driving force of Native American confederacy. After watching other tribes fail in their bids to mimic European society, the charismatic Tecumseh attempted to organize a pan-Indian alliance to put down the European encroachers. He was killed while fighting alongside the British in the War of 1812.

Sun Tzu. *The Art of War*. Translated by Samuel B. Griffith. Oxford: Oxford University Press, 1986.

Written in China more than 2,000 years ago, this is the first known study of the planning and conduct of military operations. These comprehensive essays examine not only battlefield maneuvers, but also relevant economic, political, and psychological factors. In addition to his translation, Griffith provides commentaries written by Chinese strategists, plus several essays on topics such as the influence of Sun Tzu on Mao Tse-tung and on Japanese military thought, the nature of warfare in Sun Tzu's time, and the life of Sun Tzu and other important commentators.

Vandiver, Frank E. *Black Jack: The Life and Times of John J. Pershing*. College Station: Texas A&M University Press, 1977.

Feeling that Pershing's World War I career has been adequately covered in other biographies, Vandiver takes the approach of tying Pershing's youth to his later achievements and the part he played in his time.

Weigley, Russell F. *The American Way of War: A History of United States Military Strategy and Policy*. Bloomington, IN: Indiana University Press, 1977.

Weigley examines the evolution of American military strategy from the Revolutionary War through Vietnam, defining the Civil War as a watershed in the concept of strategy and offering a critical review of the uses of sea and airpower and of strategy in a nuclear age.

About the Author

Representative Isaac Newton (Ike) Skelton IV (D–MO) has represented Missouri's Fourth Congressional District in Washington since 1977. His district includes the state capital, Jefferson City, much of the Ozark region of the state, and two major military installations—Fort Leonard Wood and Whiteman Air Force Base.

Mr. Skelton is a native of Lexington and a graduate of the Wentworth Military Academy. He received A.B. and L.L.B. degrees from the University of Missouri at Columbia, where he was named a member of Phi Beta Kappa and the Law Review. Prior to his election to Congress, Mr. Skelton served as Lafayette County Prosecuting Attorney, Missouri state attorney general, and a Missouri state senator.

A leader in the House on defense issues, Congressman Skelton is the ranking Democrat on the House Armed Services Committee. As chair of the committee's Panel on Professional Military Education in 1987–1988, he helped implement the education provisions of the Goldwater-Nichols Act. Mr. Skelton is regarded by many as the godfather of joint professional military education. In recognition of his contributions to military education, the National Defense University awarded him its first honorary degree as Doctor of National Security Affairs in 2001. As most of his district is comprised of small towns and farming communities, Congressman Skelton is also concerned about the issues of rural America. He is a former chairman of the Small Business Subcommittee on Procurement, Tourism, and Rural Development and the Congressional Rural Caucus.

Mr. Skelton is an Eagle Scout, member of Sigma Chi social fraternity, Lions Club member, and vice chairman of the Board of Trustees of the Harry S. Truman Scholarship Foundation. A member of the First Christian Church in Lexington, he and his wife Susie have three sons.

A lifelong student and avid reader of military history, Congressman Ike Skelton is an author in his own right of numerous articles published in professional military journals.